Auditing Standards 2017

Standards examinable in 2017 ICAEW ACA examinations

Wolters Kluwer

Disclaimer

This publication is sold with the understanding that neither the publisher nor the authors, with regard to this publication, are engaged in rendering legal or professional services. The material contained in this publication neither purports, nor is intended to be, advice on any particular matter.

Although this publication incorporates a considerable degree of standardisation, subjective judgment by the user, based on individual circumstances, is indispensable. This publication is an 'aid' and cannot be expected to replace such judgment.

Neither the publisher nor the authors can accept any responsibility or liability to any person, whether a purchaser of this publication or not, in respect of anything done or omitted to be done by any such person in reliance, whether sole or partial, upon the whole or any part of the contents of this publication.

© 2016 Wolters Kluwer (UK) Ltd

Wolters Kluwer
145 London Road
Kingston upon Thames
KT2 6SR

ISBN 978-1-78540-262-3

Documents in Parts One, Eight, Ten and the Glossary of Terms reproduced with the permission of the Financial Reporting Council (FRC) and the International Federation of Accountants (IFAC).

Documents in Parts Two to Seven and Nine are copyright July 2014 by the International Federation of Accountants (IFAC). All rights reserved. Used with permission of IFAC. Contact permissions@ifac.org for permission to reproduce, store or transmit, or to make other similar uses of this document.

Documents in Part Nine are Institute of Chartered Accountants of England and Wales copyright and should not be reproduced without their permission.

No responsibility for loss occasioned to any person acting or refraining from action as a result of any material in this publication can be accepted by the author or publisher.

Material is contained in this publication for which copyright is acknowledged. Permission to reproduce such material cannot be granted by the publisher and application must be made to the copyright holder.

Crown copyright is reproduced with the permission of the Controller of Her Majesty's Stationery Office.

British Library Cataloguing-in-Publication Data.

A catalogue record for this book is available from the British Library.

Typeset by Innodata Inc., India.

Printed by Druckerei C.H. Beck, Nördlingen

Auditing Standards 2017

Standards examinable in 2017 ICAEW ACA examinations

This publication is recommended for students sitting all Audit and Assurance exams in 2017.

The text may be annotated **ONLY** to the extent of underlining, sidelining and highlighting. Page tabs may be used, but must not be written on.

For more information on suggested texts and exam regulations, please visit icaew.com/exams.

Auditing Standards 2017

Standards examinable in 2017 ICAEW ACA examinations

BPP Professional Education
32-34 Colmore Circus
Birmingham B4 6BN
Phone: 0121 345 9843

Preface

Welcome to ICAEW

ICAEW is a professional membership organisation, supporting over 146,000 chartered accountants around the world. Through our technical knowledge, skills and expertise, we provide insight and leadership to the global accountancy and finance profession.

Our members provide financial knowledge and guidance based on the highest professional, technical and ethical standards. We develop and support individuals, organisations and communities to help them achieve long-term sustainable economic value.

Because of us, people can do business with confidence.

The ICAEW faculties, which include the Audit and Assurance Faculty, provide additional specialised support to faculty members in key areas and invaluable networking opportunities. Support and first-hand knowledge has never been more valuable to the audit profession and the Audit and Assurance Faculty is at the cutting edge of all audit and assurance developments. The faculty provides a comprehensive and accessible package of essential and timely guidance and technical advice which enables its members to stay ahead of the rest.

What do you get from the faculty?

Adding value to your career – the faculty will give you access to expert, exclusive and unbiased information.

Providing a single, authoritative source of information on audit and assurance – via impeccable sources from leading technical experts, a team of dedicated technical managers as well as influential volunteers working in the profession.

Staying ahead of the rest – faculty publications will provide perspectives on wider issues affecting the profession and will give you competitive advantage in the workplace.

Your voice will be heard – the faculty is ICAEW's voice on all audit and assurance related matters. In addition to its proactive work, the faculty responds to consultations, giving you the opportunity to input into developments affecting the profession.

Networking opportunities – as well as providing timely and practical guidance, our regional events can also be a useful networking opportunity.

To find out more, visit www.icaew.com/aaf.

Contents

Part Eight Other Guidance

Part Nine   IESBA and ICAEW Code of Ethics

Part Ten   FRC Ethical Standard and Glossary

Part One

International Standards on Auditing (UK)

International Standard on Auditing (UK) 200 (Revised June 2016)

Overall objectives of the independent auditor and the conduct of an audit in accordance with international standards on auditing (UK)

(Effective for audits of financial statements for periods commencing on or after 17 June 2016)

Contents

Introduction

Scope of this ISA (UK)

1   This International Standard on Auditing (UK) (ISA (UK)) deals with the independent auditor's overall responsibilities when conducting an audit of financial statements in accordance with ISAs (UK). Specifically, it sets out the overall objectives of the independent auditor, and explains the nature and scope of an audit designed to enable the independent auditor to meet those objectives. It also explains the scope, authority and structure of the ISAs (UK), and includes requirements establishing the general responsibilities of the independent auditor applicable in all audits, including the obligation to comply with the ISAs (UK). The independent auditor is referred to as 'the auditor' hereafter.

2   ISAs (UK) are written in the context of an audit of financial statements by an auditor. They are to be adapted as necessary in the circumstances when applied to audits of other historical financial information. ISAs (UK) do not address the responsibilities of the auditor that may exist in legislation, regulation or otherwise in connection with, for example, the offering of securities to the public.[1a] Such responsibilities may differ from those established in the ISAs (UK). Accordingly, while the auditor may find aspects of the ISAs (UK) helpful in such circumstances, it is the responsibility of the auditor to ensure compliance with all relevant legal, regulatory or professional obligations.

An Audit of Financial Statements

3   The purpose of an audit is to enhance the degree of confidence of intended users in the financial statements. This is achieved by the expression of an opinion by the auditor on whether the financial statements are prepared, in all material respects, in accordance with an applicable financial reporting framework. In the case of most general purpose frameworks, that opinion is on whether the financial statements are presented fairly, in all material respects, or give a true and fair view in accordance with the framework. An audit conducted in accordance with ISAs (UK) and relevant ethical requirements enables the auditor to form that opinion. (Ref: Para. A1b)

> The scope of an audit does not, however, constitute an assurance engagement with respect to the future viability of the audited entity or on the efficiency or effectiveness with which the management or administrative body has conducted or will conduct the affairs of the entity. When conducting an audit, the auditor may identify or be required to consider related matters and, where applicable, may be required to report or to communicate with management or those charged with governance or other parties on such matters in accordance with applicable laws or regulations, the ISAs (UK) or relevant ethical requirements.

4   The financial statements subject to audit are those of the entity, prepared by management of the entity with oversight from those charged with governance.[1b] ISAs (UK) do not impose responsibilities on management or those charged with governance and do not override laws and regulations that govern their responsibilities. However, an audit in

---

[1a] *In the UK, standards and guidance for accountants undertaking engagements in connection with an investment circular are set out in the FRC's Standards for Investment Reporting (SIRS).*

[1b] *In the UK, those charged with governance are responsible for the preparation of the financial statements. For corporate entities, directors have a collective responsibility; those charged with governance of other types of entity may also have a collective responsibility established in applicable law or regulation or under the terms of their appointment.*

accordance with ISAs (UK) is conducted on the premise that management and, where appropriate, those charged with governance have acknowledged certain responsibilities that are fundamental to the conduct of the audit. The audit of the financial statements does not relieve management or those charged with governance of their responsibilities. (Ref: Para. A2–A11)

As the basis for the auditor's opinion, ISAs (UK) require the auditor to obtain reasonable   5
assurance about whether the financial statements as a whole are free from material misstatement, whether due to fraud or error. Reasonable assurance is a high level of assurance. It is obtained when the auditor has obtained sufficient appropriate audit evidence to reduce audit risk (that is, the risk that the auditor expresses an inappropriate opinion when the financial statements are materially misstated) to an acceptably low level. However, reasonable assurance is not an absolute level of assurance, because there are inherent limitations of an audit which result in most of the audit evidence on which the auditor draws conclusions and bases the auditor's opinion being persuasive rather than conclusive. (Ref: Para. A28–A52)

The concept of materiality is applied by the auditor both in planning and performing the   6
audit, and in evaluating the effect of identified misstatements on the audit and of uncorrected misstatements, if any, on the financial statements.[1] In general, misstatements, including omissions, are considered to be material if, individually or in the aggregate, they could reasonably be expected to influence the economic decisions of users taken on the basis of the financial statements. Judgments about materiality are made in the light of surrounding circumstances, and are affected by the auditor's perception of the financial information needs of users of the financial statements, and by the size or nature of a misstatement, or a combination of both. The auditor's opinion deals with the financial statements as a whole and therefore the auditor is not responsible for the detection of misstatements that are not material to the financial statements as a whole.

The ISAs (UK) contain objectives, requirements and application and other explanatory   7
material that are designed to support the auditor in obtaining reasonable assurance. The ISAs (UK) require that the auditor exercise professional judgment and maintain professional skepticism throughout the planning and performance of the audit and, among other things:

- Identify and assess risks of material misstatement, whether due to fraud or error, based on an understanding of the entity and its environment, including the entity's internal control.
- Obtain sufficient appropriate audit evidence about whether material misstatements exist, through designing and implementing appropriate responses to the assessed risks.
- Form an opinion on the financial statements based on conclusions drawn from the audit evidence obtained.

The form of opinion expressed by the auditor will depend upon the applicable financial   8
reporting framework and any applicable law or regulation. (Ref: Para. A12–A13)

The auditor may also have certain other communication and reporting responsibilities   9
to users, management, those charged with governance, or parties outside the entity, in relation to matters arising from the audit. These may be established by the ISAs (UK) or by applicable law or regulation.[2]

---

[1] *ISA (UK) 320 (Revised June 2016)*, Materiality in Planning and Performing an Audit *and ISA (UK) 450 (Revised June 2016)*, Evaluation of Misstatements Identified during the Audit.

[2] *See, for example, ISA (UK) 260 (Revised June 2016)*, Communication with Those Charged with Governance; *and paragraph 43 of ISA (UK) 240 (Revised June 2016)*, The Auditor's Responsibilities Relating to Fraud in an Audit of Financial Statements.

Effective Date

10   This ISA (UK) is effective for audits of financial statements for periods commencing on or after 17 June 2016. Earlier adoption is permitted.

Overall Objectives of the Auditor

11   In conducting an audit of financial statements, the overall objectives of the auditor are:

(a)   To obtain reasonable assurance about whether the financial statements as a whole are free from material misstatement, whether due to fraud or error, thereby enabling the auditor to express an opinion on whether the financial statements are prepared, in all material respects, in accordance with an applicable financial reporting framework; and

(b)   To report on the financial statements, and communicate as required by the ISAs (UK), in accordance with the auditor's findings.

12   In all cases when reasonable assurance cannot be obtained and a qualified opinion in the auditor's report is insufficient in the circumstances for purposes of reporting to the intended users of the financial statements, the ISAs (UK) require that the auditor disclaim an opinion or withdraw (or resign)[3] from the engagement, where withdrawal is possible under applicable law or regulation.

Definitions

13   For purposes of the ISAs (UK), the following terms have the meanings attributed below:

(a)   Applicable financial reporting framework – The financial reporting framework adopted by management and, where appropriate, those charged with governance in the preparation of the financial statements that is acceptable in view of the nature of the entity and the objective of the financial statements, or that is required by law or regulation.

The term 'fair presentation framework' is used to refer to a financial reporting framework that requires compliance with the requirements of the framework and:

(i)   Acknowledges explicitly or implicitly that, to achieve fair presentation of the financial statements, it may be necessary for management to provide disclosures beyond those specifically required by the framework; or

(ii)   Acknowledges explicitly that it may be necessary for management to depart from a requirement of the framework to achieve fair presentation of the financial statements. Such departures are expected to be necessary only in extremely rare circumstances.

The term 'compliance framework' is used to refer to a financial reporting framework that requires compliance with the requirements of the framework, but does not contain the acknowledgements in (i) or (ii) above.

In the UK, the applicable financial reporting framework includes the requirements of applicable law.

(b)   Audit evidence – Information used by the auditor in arriving at the conclusions on which the auditor's opinion is based. Audit evidence includes both information contained in the accounting records underlying the financial statements and other information. For purposes of the ISAs (UK):

(i)   Sufficiency of audit evidence is the measure of the quantity of audit evidence. The quantity of the audit evidence needed is affected by the auditor's assessment of the risks of material misstatement and also by the quality of such audit evidence.

---

[3]   *In the ISAs (UK), only the term 'withdrawal' is used.*

    (ii)   Appropriateness of audit evidence is the measure of the quality of audit evidence; that is, its relevance and its reliability in providing support for the conclusions on which the auditor's opinion is based.

(c)   Audit risk – The risk that the auditor expresses an inappropriate audit opinion when the financial statements are materially misstated. Audit risk is a function of the risks of material misstatement and detection risk.

(d)   Auditor – 'Auditor' is used to refer to the person or persons conducting the audit, usually the engagement partner or other members of the engagement team,[3a] or, as applicable, the firm. Where an ISA (UK) expressly intends that a requirement or responsibility be fulfilled by the engagement partner, the term 'engagement partner' rather than 'auditor' is used. 'Engagement partner' and 'firm' are to be read as referring to their public sector equivalents where relevant.

(e)   Detection risk – The risk that the procedures performed by the auditor to reduce audit risk to an acceptably low level will not detect a misstatement that exists and that could be material, either individually or when aggregated with other misstatements.

(f)   Financial statements – A structured representation of historical financial information, including disclosures, intended to communicate an entity's economic resources or obligations at a point in time or the changes therein for a period of time in accordance with a financial reporting framework. The term 'financial statements' ordinarily refers to a complete set of financial statements as determined by the requirements of the applicable financial reporting framework, but can also refer to a single financial statement. Disclosures comprise explanatory or descriptive information, set out as required, expressly permitted or otherwise allowed by the applicable financial reporting framework, on the face of a financial statement, or in the notes, or incorporated therein by cross-reference. (Ref: Para. A1–A1a)

(g)   Historical financial information – Information expressed in financial terms in relation to a particular entity, derived primarily from that entity's accounting system, about economic events occurring in past time periods or about economic conditions or circumstances at points in time in the past.

(h)   Management – The person(s) with executive responsibility for the conduct of the entity's operations. For some entities in some jurisdictions, management includes some or all of those charged with governance, for example, executive members of a governance board, or an owner-manager.

In the UK, management will not normally include non-executive directors.

(i)   Misstatement – A difference between the amount, classification, presentation, or disclosure of a reported financial statement item and the amount, classification, presentation, or disclosure that is required for the item to be in accordance with the applicable financial reporting framework. Misstatements can arise from error or fraud.

    Where the auditor expresses an opinion on whether the financial statements are presented fairly, in all material respects, or give a true and fair view, misstatements also include those adjustments of amounts, classifications, presentation, or disclosures that, in the auditor's judgment, are necessary for the financial statements to be presented fairly, in all material respects, or to give a true and fair view.

(j)   Premise, relating to the responsibilities of management and, where appropriate, those charged with governance, on which an audit is conducted – That management and, where appropriate, those charged with governance have acknowledged and understand that they have the following responsibilities that are fundamental to the conduct of an audit in accordance with ISAs (UK). That is, responsibility:

[3a] *In the UK, this includes the key audit partner as defined in ISA (UK) 220 (Revised June 2016),* Quality Control for an Audit of Financial Statements, *paragraph 7D-1(d).*

> (i) For the preparation of the financial statements in accordance with the applicable financial reporting framework, including where relevant their fair presentation;
>
> (ii) For such internal control as management and, where appropriate, those charged with governance determine is necessary to enable the preparation of financial statements that are free from material misstatement, whether due to fraud or error; and
>
> (iii) To provide the auditor with:
>
>   a.   Access to all information of which management and, where appropriate, those charged with governance are aware that is relevant to the preparation of the financial statements such as records, documentation and other matters;
>
>   b.   Additional information that the auditor may request from management and, where appropriate, those charged with governance for the purpose of the audit; and
>
>   c.   Unrestricted access to persons within the entity from whom the auditor determines it necessary to obtain audit evidence.
>
> In the case of a fair presentation framework, (i) above may be restated as 'for the preparation and *fair* presentation of the financial statements in accordance with the financial reporting framework,' or 'for the preparation of financial statements *that give a true and fair view* in accordance with the financial reporting framework.'
>
> The 'premise, relating to the responsibilities of management and, where appropriate, those charged with governance, on which an audit is conducted' may also be referred to as the 'premise.'

(k) Professional judgment – The application of relevant training, knowledge and experience, within the context provided by auditing, accounting and ethical standards, in making informed decisions about the courses of action that are appropriate in the circumstances of the audit engagement.

(l) Professional skepticism – An attitude that includes a questioning mind, being alert to conditions which may indicate possible misstatement due to error or fraud, and a critical assessment of audit evidence.

(m) Reasonable assurance – In the context of an audit of financial statements, a high, but not absolute, level of assurance.

(n) Risk of material misstatement – The risk that the financial statements are materially misstated prior to audit. This consists of two components, described as follows at the assertion level:

> (i) Inherent risk – The susceptibility of an assertion about a class of transaction, account balance or disclosure to a misstatement that could be material, either individually or when aggregated with other misstatements, before consideration of any related controls.
>
> (ii) Control risk – The risk that a misstatement that could occur in an assertion about a class of transaction, account balance or disclosure and that could be material, either individually or when aggregated with other misstatements, will not be prevented, or detected and corrected, on a timely basis by the entity's internal control.

(o) Those charged with governance – The person(s) or organization(s) (for example, a corporate trustee) with responsibility for overseeing the strategic direction of the entity and obligations related to the accountability of the entity. This includes overseeing the financial reporting process. For some entities in some jurisdictions, those charged with governance may include management personnel, for example, executive members of a governance board of a private or public sector entity, or an owner-manager.

In the UK, those charged with governance include the directors (executive and non-executive) of a company and the members of an audit committee where one exists. For other types of entity it usually includes equivalent persons such as the partners, proprietors, committee of management or trustees.

Requirements

Ethical Requirements Relating to an Audit of Financial Statements

The auditor shall comply with relevant ethical requirements, including those pertaining to   **14**
independence, relating to financial statement audit engagements. (Ref: Para. A14–A17)

Professional Skepticism

The auditor shall plan and perform an audit with professional skepticism recognizing that   **15**
circumstances may exist that cause the financial statements to be materially misstated.
(Ref: Para. A18–A22)

In the UK, the auditor shall maintain professional skepticism throughout the audit, recognising the possibility of a material misstatement due to facts or behaviour indicating irregularities, including fraud, or error, notwithstanding the auditor's past experience of the honesty and integrity of the entity's management and of those charged with governance.

Professional Judgment

The auditor shall exercise professional judgment in planning and performing an audit of   **16**
financial statements. (Ref: Para. A23–A27)

Sufficient Appropriate Audit Evidence and Audit Risk

To obtain reasonable assurance, the auditor shall obtain sufficient appropriate audit   **17**
evidence to reduce audit risk to an acceptably low level and thereby enable the auditor to
draw reasonable conclusions on which to base the auditor's opinion. (Ref: Para. A28–A52)

Conduct of an Audit in Accordance with ISAs (UK)

Complying with ISAs (UK) Relevant to the Audit

The auditor shall comply with all ISAs (UK) relevant to the audit. An ISA (UK) is relevant   **18**
to the audit when the ISA (UK) is in effect and the circumstances addressed by the ISA
(UK) exist. (Ref: Para. A53–A57)

The auditor shall have an understanding of the entire text of an ISA (UK), including its   **19**
application and other explanatory material, to understand its objectives and to apply its
requirements properly. (Ref: Para. A58–A66)

The auditor shall not represent compliance with ISAs (UK) in the auditor's report unless   **20**
the auditor has complied with the requirements of this ISA (UK) and all other ISAs (UK)
relevant to the audit.

Objectives Stated in Individual ISAs (UK)

21   To achieve the overall objectives of the auditor, the auditor shall use the objectives stated in relevant ISAs (UK) in planning and performing the audit, having regard to the interrelationships among the ISAs (UK), to: (Ref: Para. A67–A69)

(a) Determine whether any audit procedures in addition to those required by the ISAs (UK) are necessary in pursuance of the objectives stated in the ISAs (UK); and (Ref: Para. A70)

(b) Evaluate whether sufficient appropriate audit evidence has been obtained. (Ref: Para. A71)

Complying with Relevant Requirements

22   Subject to paragraph 23, the auditor shall comply with each requirement of an ISA (UK) unless, in the circumstances of the audit:

(a) The entire ISA (UK) is not relevant; or

(b) The requirement is not relevant because it is conditional and the condition does not exist. (Ref: Para. A72–A73)

23   In exceptional circumstances, the auditor may judge it necessary to depart from a relevant requirement in an ISA (UK). In such circumstances, the auditor shall perform alternative audit procedures to achieve the aim of that requirement. The need for the auditor to depart from a relevant requirement is expected to arise only where the requirement is for a specific procedure to be performed and, in the specific circumstances of the audit, that procedure would be ineffective in achieving the aim of the requirement. (Ref: Para. A74)

Failure to Achieve an Objective

24   If an objective in a relevant ISA (UK) cannot be achieved, the auditor shall evaluate whether this prevents the auditor from achieving the overall objectives of the auditor and thereby requires the auditor, in accordance with the ISAs (UK), to modify the auditor's opinion or withdraw from the engagement (where withdrawal is possible under applicable law or regulation). Failure to achieve an objective represents a significant matter requiring documentation in accordance with ISA (UK) 230 (Revised June 2016).[4] (Ref: Para. A75–A76)

***

Application and Other Explanatory Material

Definitions

Financial Statements (Ref: Para. 13(f))

A1   Some financial reporting frameworks may refer to an entity's economic resources or obligations in other terms. For example, these may be referred to as the entity's assets and liabilities, and the residual difference between them may be referred to as equity or equity interests.

---

[4] *ISA (UK) 230 (Revised June 2016)*, Audit Documentation, *paragraph 8(c)*.

Explanatory or descriptive information required to be included in the financial statements   **A1a**
by the applicable financial reporting framework may be incorporated therein by cross-
reference to information in another document, such as a management report or a risk
report. 'Incorporated therein by cross-reference' means cross-referenced from the financial
statements to the other document, but not from the other document to the financial
statements, Where the applicable financial reporting framework does not expressly
prohibit the cross-referencing of where explanatory or descriptive information may be
found, and the information has been appropriately cross-referenced, the information will
form part of the financial statements.

An Audit of Financial Statements

Scope of the Audit (Ref: Para. 3)

The auditor's opinion on the financial statements deals with whether the financial   **A1b**
statements are prepared, in all material respects, in accordance with the applicable financial
reporting framework. Such an opinion is common to all audits of financial statements. The
auditor's opinion therefore does not assure, for example, the future viability of the entity
nor the efficiency or effectiveness with which management has conducted the affairs of the
entity. In some jurisdictions, however, applicable law or regulation may require auditors to
provide opinions on other specific matters, such as the effectiveness of internal control, or
the consistency of a separate management report with the financial statements. While the
ISAs (UK) include requirements and guidance in relation to such matters to the extent that
they are relevant to forming an opinion on the financial statements, the auditor would be
required to undertake further work if the auditor had additional responsibilities to provide
such opinions.

Preparation of the Financial Statements (Ref: Para. 4)

Law or regulation may establish the responsibilities of management and, where   **A2**
appropriate, those charged with governance in relation to financial reporting. However,
the extent of these responsibilities, or the way in which they are described, may differ
across jurisdictions. Despite these differences, an audit in accordance with ISAs (UK) is
conducted on the premise that management and, where appropriate, those charged with
governance have acknowledged and understand that they have responsibility:

(a)   For the preparation of the financial statements in accordance with the applicable
      financial reporting framework, including where relevant their fair presentation;
(b)   For such internal control as management and, where appropriate, those charged with
      governance determine is necessary to enable the preparation of financial statements
      that are free from material misstatement, whether due to fraud or error; and
(c)   To provide the auditor with:
      (i)   Access to all information of which management and, where appropriate, those
             charged with governance are aware that is relevant to the preparation of the
             financial statements such as records, documentation and other matters;
      (ii)   Additional information that the auditor may request from management and,
             where appropriate, those charged with governance for the purpose of the audit;
             and
      (iii) Unrestricted access to persons within the entity from whom the auditor
             determines it necessary to obtain audit evidence.

The preparation of the financial statements by management and, where appropriate, those   **A3**
charged with governance requires:

- The identification of the applicable financial reporting framework, in the context of any relevant laws or regulations.
- The preparation of the financial statements in accordance with that framework.
- The inclusion of an adequate description of that framework in the financial statements.

The preparation of the financial statements requires management to exercise judgment in making accounting estimates that are reasonable in the circumstances, as well as to select and apply appropriate accounting policies. These judgments are made in the context of the applicable financial reporting framework.

A4   The financial statements may be prepared in accordance with a financial reporting framework designed to meet:

- The common financial information needs of a wide range of users (that is, 'general purpose financial statements'); or
- The financial information needs of specific users (that is, 'special purpose financial statements').

A5   The applicable financial reporting framework often encompasses financial reporting standards established by an authorized or recognized standards setting organization, or legislative or regulatory requirements. In some cases, the financial reporting framework may encompass both financial reporting standards established by an authorized or recognized standards setting organization and legislative or regulatory requirements. Other sources may provide direction on the application of the applicable financial reporting framework. In some cases, the applicable financial reporting framework may encompass such other sources, or may even consist only of such sources. Such other sources may include:

- The legal and ethical environment, including statutes, regulations, court decisions, and professional ethical obligations in relation to accounting matters;
- Published accounting interpretations of varying authority issued by standards setting, professional or regulatory organizations;
- Published views of varying authority on emerging accounting issues issued by standards setting, professional or regulatory organizations;
- General and industry practices widely recognized and prevalent; and
- Accounting literature.

Where conflicts exist between the financial reporting framework and the sources from which direction on its application may be obtained, or among the sources that encompass the financial reporting framework, the source with the highest authority prevails.

A6   The requirements of the applicable financial reporting framework determine the form and content of the financial statements. Although the framework may not specify how to account for or disclose all transactions or events, it ordinarily embodies sufficient broad principles that can serve as a basis for developing and applying accounting policies that are consistent with the concepts underlying the requirements of the framework.

A7   Some financial reporting frameworks are fair presentation frameworks, while others are compliance frameworks. Financial reporting frameworks that encompass primarily the financial reporting standards established by an organization that is authorized or recognized to promulgate standards to be used by entities for preparing general purpose financial statements are often designed to achieve fair presentation, for example, International Financial Reporting Standards (IFRSs) issued by the International Accounting Standards Board (IASB).

The requirements of the applicable financial reporting framework also determine what   **A8**
constitutes a complete set of financial statements. In the case of many frameworks,
financial statements are intended to provide information about the financial position,
financial performance and cash flows of an entity. For such frameworks, a complete set
of financial statements would include a balance sheet; an income statement; a statement
of changes in equity; a cash flow statement; and related notes. For some other financial
reporting frameworks, a single financial statement and the related notes might constitute a
complete set of financial statements:

- For example, the International Public Sector Accounting Standard (IPSAS),
  'Financial Reporting Under the Cash Basis of Accounting' issued by the International
  Public Sector Accounting Standards Board states that the primary financial statement
  is a statement of cash receipts and payments when a public sector entity prepares its
  financial statements in accordance with that IPSAS.
- Other examples of a single financial statement, each of which would include related
  notes, are:
  - Balance sheet.
  - Statement of income or statement of operations.
  - Statement of retained earnings.
  - Statement of cash flows.
  - Statement of assets and liabilities that does not include owner's equity.
  - Statement of changes in owners' equity.
  - Statement of revenue and expenses.
  - Statement of operations by product lines.

ISA (UK) 210 (Revised June 2016) establishes requirements and provides guidance on   **A9**
determining the acceptability of the applicable financial reporting framework.[5] ISA 800
deals with special considerations when financial statements are prepared in accordance
with a special purpose framework.[6]

Because of the significance of the premise to the conduct of an audit, the auditor is   **A10**
required to obtain the agreement of management and, where appropriate, those charged
with governance that they acknowledge and understand that they have the responsibilities
set out in paragraph A2 as a precondition for accepting the audit engagement.[7]

Considerations Specific to Audits in the Public Sector

The mandates for audits of the financial statements of public sector entities may be   **A11**
broader than those of other entities. As a result, the premise, relating to management's
responsibilities, on which an audit of the financial statements of a public sector entity
is conducted may include additional responsibilities, such as the responsibility for the
execution of transactions and events in accordance with law, regulation or other authority.[8]

---

[5] *ISA (UK) 210 (Revised June 2016)*, Agreeing the Terms of Audit Engagements, *paragraph 6(a).*

[6] *ISA 800*, Special Considerations—Audits of Financial Statements Prepared in Accordance with Special Purpose
Frameworks, *paragraph 8.*
ISA 800 has not been promulgated by the FRC for application in the UK.

[7] *ISA (UK) 210 (Revised June 2016), paragraph 6(b).*

[8] *See paragraph A57.*

Form of the Auditor's Opinion (Ref: Para. 8)

A12   The opinion expressed by the auditor is on whether the financial statements are prepared, in all material respects, in accordance with the applicable financial reporting framework. The form of the auditor's opinion, however, will depend upon the applicable financial reporting framework and any applicable law or regulation. Most financial reporting frameworks include requirements relating to the presentation of the financial statements; for such frameworks, *preparation* of the financial statements in accordance with the applicable financial reporting framework includes *presentation*.

A13   Where the financial reporting framework is a fair presentation framework, as is generally the case for general purpose financial statements, the opinion required by the ISAs (UK) is on whether the financial statements are presented fairly, in all material respects, or give a true and fair view. Where the financial reporting framework is a compliance framework, the opinion required is on whether the financial statements are prepared, in all material respects, in accordance with the framework. Unless specifically stated otherwise, references in the ISAs (UK) to the auditor's opinion cover both forms of opinion.

Ethical Requirements Relating to an Audit of Financial Statements
(Ref: Para. 14)

A14   The auditor is subject to relevant ethical requirements, including those pertaining to independence, relating to financial statement audit engagements. Relevant ethical requirements ordinarily comprise Parts A and B of the International Ethics Standards Board of Accountants' *Code of Ethics for Professional Accountants* (the IESBA Code) related to an audit of financial statements together with national requirements that are more restrictive.

A14-1   In the UK, auditors are subject to ethical requirements from two sources: the FRC's Ethical Standard concerning the integrity, objectivity and independence of the auditor, and the ethical pronouncements established by the auditor's relevant professional body.

A15   Part A of the IESBA Code establishes the fundamental principles of professional ethics relevant to the auditor when conducting an audit of financial statements and provides a conceptual framework for applying those principles. The fundamental principles with which the auditor is required to comply by the IESBA Code are:

(a) Integrity;
(b) Objectivity;
(c) Professional competence and due care;
(d) Confidentiality; and
(e) Professional behavior.

Part B of the IESBA Code illustrates how the conceptual framework is to be applied in specific situations.

A16   In the case of an audit engagement it is in the public interest and, therefore, required by the IESBA Code, that the auditor be independent of the entity subject to the audit. The IESBA Code describes independence as comprising both independence of mind and independence in appearance. The auditor's independence from the entity safeguards the auditor's ability to form an audit opinion without being affected by influences that might compromise that opinion. Independence enhances the auditor's ability to act with integrity, to be objective and to maintain an attitude of professional skepticism.

International Standard on Quality Control (ISQC) (UK) 1 (Revised June 2016)[9], or   **A17**
national requirements that are at least as demanding,[10] deal with the firm's responsibilities
to establish and maintain its system of quality control for audit engagements. ISQC (UK)
1 (Revised June 2016) sets out the responsibilities of the firm for establishing policies and
procedures designed to provide it with reasonable assurance that the firm and its personnel
comply with relevant ethical requirements, including those pertaining to independence.[11]
ISA (UK) 220 (Revised June 2016) sets out the engagement partner's responsibilities
with respect to relevant ethical requirements. These include remaining alert, through
observation and making inquiries as necessary, for evidence of non-compliance with
relevant ethical requirements by members of the engagement team, determining the
appropriate action if matters come to the engagement partner's attention that indicate that
members of the engagement team have not complied with relevant ethical requirements,
and forming a conclusion on compliance with independence requirements that apply to the
audit engagement.[12] ISA (UK) 220 (Revised June 2016) recognizes that the engagement
team is entitled to rely on a firm's system of quality control in meeting its responsibilities
with respect to quality control procedures applicable to the individual audit engagement,
unless information provided by the firm or other parties suggests otherwise.

Professional Skepticism (Ref: Para. 15)

Professional skepticism includes being alert to, for example: **A18**

- Audit evidence that contradicts other audit evidence obtained.
- Information that brings into question the reliability of documents and responses to
  inquiries to be used as audit evidence.
- Conditions that may indicate possible fraud.
- Circumstances that suggest the need for audit procedures in addition to those required
  by the ISAs (UK).

Maintaining professional skepticism throughout the audit is necessary if the auditor is, for   **A19**
example, to reduce the risks of:

- Overlooking unusual circumstances.
- Over generalizing when drawing conclusions from audit observations.
- Using inappropriate assumptions in determining the nature, timing, and extent of the
  audit procedures and evaluating the results thereof.

Professional skepticism is necessary to the critical assessment of audit evidence. This   **A20**
includes questioning contradictory audit evidence and the reliability of documents and
responses to inquiries and other information obtained from management and those charged
with governance. It also includes consideration of the sufficiency and appropriateness of
audit evidence obtained in the light of the circumstances, for example in the case where
fraud risk factors exist and a single document, of a nature that is susceptible to fraud, is the
sole supporting evidence for a material financial statement amount.

The auditor may accept records and documents as genuine unless the auditor has reason   **A21**
to believe the contrary. Nevertheless, the auditor is required to consider the reliability

---

[9] *International Standard on Quality Control (ISQC) (UK) 1 (Revised June 2016),* Quality Control for Firms that
Perform Audits and Reviews of Financial Statements, and Other Assurance and Related Services Engagements.

[10] *ISA (UK) 220 (Revised June 2016),* Quality Control for an Audit of Financial Statements, *paragraph 2.*

[11] *ISQC (UK) 1 (Revised June 2016), paragraphs 20–25.*

[12] *ISA (UK) 220 (Revised June 2016), paragraphs 9–11.*

of information to be used as audit evidence.[13] In cases of doubt about the reliability of information or indications of possible fraud (for example, if conditions identified during the audit cause the auditor to believe that a document may not be authentic or that terms in a document may have been falsified), the ISAs (UK) require that the auditor investigate further and determine what modifications or additions to audit procedures are necessary to resolve the matter.[14]

A22   The auditor cannot be expected to disregard past experience of the honesty and integrity of the entity's management and those charged with governance. Nevertheless, a belief that management and those charged with governance are honest and have integrity does not relieve the auditor of the need to maintain professional skepticism or allow the auditor to be satisfied with less-than-persuasive audit evidence when obtaining reasonable assurance.

Professional Judgment (Ref: Para. 16)

A23   Professional judgment is essential to the proper conduct of an audit. This is because interpretation of relevant ethical requirements and the ISAs (UK) and the informed decisions required throughout the audit cannot be made without the application of relevant knowledge and experience to the facts and circumstances. Professional judgment is necessary in particular regarding decisions about:

- Materiality and audit risk.
- The nature, timing, and extent of audit procedures used to meet the requirements of the ISAs (UK) and gather audit evidence.
- Evaluating whether sufficient appropriate audit evidence has been obtained, and whether more needs to be done to achieve the objectives of the ISAs (UK) and thereby, the overall objectives of the auditor.
- The evaluation of management's judgments in applying the entity's applicable financial reporting framework.
- The drawing of conclusions based on the audit evidence obtained, for example, assessing the reasonableness of the estimates made by management in preparing the financial statements.

A24   The distinguishing feature of the professional judgment expected of an auditor is that it is exercised by an auditor whose training, knowledge and experience have assisted in developing the necessary competencies to achieve reasonable judgments.

A25   The exercise of professional judgment in any particular case is based on the facts and circumstances that are known by the auditor. Consultation on difficult or contentious matters during the course of the audit, both within the engagement team and between the engagement team and others at the appropriate level within or outside the firm, such as that required by ISA (UK) 220 (Revised June 2016),[15] assist the auditor in making informed and reasonable judgments.

A26   Professional judgment can be evaluated based on whether the judgment reached reflects a competent application of auditing and accounting principles and is appropriate in the light of, and consistent with, the facts and circumstances that were known to the auditor up to the date of the auditor's report.

---

[13]   *ISA (UK) 500*, Audit Evidence, *paragraphs 7–9.*

[14]   *ISA (UK) 240 (Revised June 2016), paragraph 13; ISA (UK) 500, paragraph 11; ISA (UK) 505,* External Confirmations, *paragraphs 10–11, and 16.*

[15]   *ISA (UK) 220 (Revised June 2016), paragraph 18.*

Professional judgment needs to be exercised throughout the audit. It also needs to   **A27**
be appropriately documented. In this regard, the auditor is required to prepare audit
documentation sufficient to enable an experienced auditor, having no previous connection
with the audit, to understand the significant professional judgments made in reaching
conclusions on significant matters arising during the audit.[16] Professional judgment is not
to be used as the justification for decisions that are not otherwise supported by the facts
and circumstances of the engagement or sufficient appropriate audit evidence.

Sufficient Appropriate Audit Evidence and Audit Risk (Ref: Para. 5 and 17)

Sufficiency and Appropriateness of Audit Evidence

Audit evidence is necessary to support the auditor's opinion and report. It is cumulative   **A28**
in nature and is primarily obtained from audit procedures performed during the course
of the audit. It may, however, also include information obtained from other sources
such as previous audits (provided the auditor has determined whether changes have
occurred since the previous audit that may affect its relevance to the current audit[17]) or
a firm's quality control procedures for client acceptance and continuance. In addition
to other sources inside and outside the entity, the entity's accounting records are an
important source of audit evidence. Also, information that may be used as audit evidence
may have been prepared by an expert employed or engaged by the entity. Audit evidence
comprises both information that supports and corroborates management's assertions,
and any information that contradicts such assertions. In addition, in some cases, the
absence of information (for example, management's refusal to provide a requested
representation) is used by the auditor, and therefore, also constitutes audit evidence.
Most of the auditor's work in forming the auditor's opinion consists of obtaining and
evaluating audit evidence.

The sufficiency and appropriateness of audit evidence are interrelated. Sufficiency is   **A29**
the measure of the quantity of audit evidence. The quantity of audit evidence needed is
affected by the auditor's assessment of the risks of misstatement (the higher the assessed
risks, the more audit evidence is likely to be required) and also by the quality of such audit
evidence (the higher the quality, the less may be required). Obtaining more audit evidence,
however, may not compensate for its poor quality.

Appropriateness is the measure of the quality of audit evidence; that is, its relevance and its   **A30**
reliability in providing support for the conclusions on which the auditor's opinion is based.
The reliability of evidence is influenced by its source and by its nature, and is dependent
on the individual circumstances under which it is obtained.

Whether sufficient appropriate audit evidence has been obtained to reduce audit risk to   **A31**
an acceptably low level, and thereby enable the auditor to draw reasonable conclusions
on which to base the auditor's opinion, is a matter of professional judgment. ISA (UK)
500 and other relevant ISAs (UK) establish additional requirements and provide further
guidance applicable throughout the audit regarding the auditor's considerations in obtaining
sufficient appropriate audit evidence.

---

[16] *ISA (UK) 230 (Revised June 2016), paragraph 8.*

[17] *ISA (UK) 315 (Revised June 2016)*, Identifying and Assessing the Risks of Material Misstatement through Understanding the Entity and Its Environment, *paragraph 9.*

Audit Risk

A32   Audit risk is a function of the risks of material misstatement and detection risk. The assessment of risks is based on audit procedures to obtain information necessary for that purpose and evidence obtained throughout the audit. The assessment of risks is a matter of professional judgment, rather than a matter capable of precise measurement.

A33   For purposes of the ISAs (UK), audit risk does not include the risk that the auditor might express an opinion that the financial statements are materially misstated when they are not. This risk is ordinarily insignificant. Further, audit risk is a technical term related to the process of auditing; it does not refer to the auditor's business risks such as loss from litigation, adverse publicity, or other events arising in connection with the audit of financial statements.

Risks of Material Misstatement

A34   The risks of material misstatement may exist at two levels:

- The overall financial statement level; and
- The assertion level for classes of transactions, account balances, and disclosures.

A35   Risks of material misstatement at the overall financial statement level refer to risks of material misstatement that relate pervasively to the financial statements as a whole and potentially affect many assertions.

A36   Risks of material misstatement at the assertion level are assessed in order to determine the nature, timing, and extent of further audit procedures necessary to obtain sufficient appropriate audit evidence. This evidence enables the auditor to express an opinion on the financial statements at an acceptably low level of audit risk. Auditors use various approaches to accomplish the objective of assessing the risks of material misstatement. For example, the auditor may make use of a model that expresses the general relationship of the components of audit risk in mathematical terms to arrive at an acceptable level of detection risk. Some auditors find such a model to be useful when planning audit procedures.

A37   The risks of material misstatement at the assertion level consist of two components: inherent risk and control risk. Inherent risk and control risk are the entity's risks; they exist independently of the audit of the financial statements.

A38   Inherent risk is higher for some assertions and related classes of transactions, account balances, and disclosures than for others. For example, it may be higher for complex calculations or for accounts consisting of amounts derived from accounting estimates that are subject to significant estimation uncertainty. External circumstances giving rise to business risks may also influence inherent risk. For example, technological developments might make a particular product obsolete, thereby causing inventory to be more susceptible to overstatement. Factors in the entity and its environment that relate to several or all of the classes of transactions, account balances, or disclosures may also influence the inherent risk related to a specific assertion. Such factors may include, for example, a lack of sufficient working capital to continue operations or a declining industry characterized by a large number of business failures.

A39   Control risk is a function of the effectiveness of the design, implementation and maintenance of internal control by management to address identified risks that threaten the achievement of the entity's objectives relevant to preparation of the entity's financial statements. However, internal control, no matter how well designed and operated, can only reduce, but not eliminate, risks of material misstatement in the financial statements, because of the inherent limitations of internal control. These include, for example, the possibility of human errors or mistakes, or of controls being circumvented by collusion or inappropriate management override. Accordingly, some control risk will always exist. The ISAs (UK) provide the conditions under which the auditor is required to, or may choose to, test the operating effectiveness of controls in determining the nature, timing and extent of substantive procedures to be performed.[18]

The ISAs (UK) do not ordinarily refer to inherent risk and control risk separately, but rather   **A40** to a combined assessment of the 'risks of material misstatement.' However, the auditor may make separate or combined assessments of inherent and control risk depending on preferred audit techniques or methodologies and practical considerations. The assessment of the risks of material misstatement may be expressed in quantitative terms, such as in percentages, or in non-quantitative terms. In any case, the need for the auditor to make appropriate risk assessments is more important than the different approaches by which they may be made.

ISA (UK) 315 (Revised June 2016) establishes requirements and provides guidance on   **A41** identifying and assessing the risks of material misstatement at the financial statement and assertion levels.

Detection Risk

For a given level of audit risk, the acceptable level of detection risk bears an inverse   **A42** relationship to the assessed risks of material misstatement at the assertion level. For example, the greater the risks of material misstatement the auditor believes exists, the less the detection risk that can be accepted and, accordingly, the more persuasive the audit evidence required by the auditor.

Detection risk relates to the nature, timing, and extent of the auditor's procedures that are   **A43** determined by the auditor to reduce audit risk to an acceptably low level. It is therefore a function of the effectiveness of an audit procedure and of its application by the auditor. Matters such as:

- adequate planning;
- proper assignment of personnel to the engagement team;
- the application of professional scepticism; and
- supervision and review of the audit work performed,

assist to enhance the effectiveness of an audit procedure and of its application and reduce the possibility that an auditor might select an inappropriate audit procedure, misapply an appropriate audit procedure, or misinterpret the audit results.

ISA (UK) 300 (Revised June 2016)[19] and ISA (UK) 330 (Revised June 2016) establish   **A44** requirements and provide guidance on planning an audit of financial statements and the auditor's responses to assessed risks. Detection risk, however, can only be reduced, not eliminated, because of the inherent limitations of an audit. Accordingly, some detection risk will always exist.

---

[18] *ISA (UK) 330 (Revised June 2016),* The Auditor's Reponses to Assessed Risks, *paragraphs 7–17.*

[19] *ISA (UK) 300 (Revised June 2016),* Planning an Audit of Financial Statements.

Inherent Limitations of an Audit

A45   The auditor is not expected to, and cannot, reduce audit risk to zero and cannot therefore obtain absolute assurance that the financial statements are free from material misstatement due to fraud or error. This is because there are inherent limitations of an audit, which result in most of the audit evidence on which the auditor draws conclusions and bases the auditor's opinion being persuasive rather than conclusive. The inherent limitations of an audit arise from:

- The nature of financial reporting;
- The nature of audit procedures; and
- The need for the audit to be conducted within a reasonable period of time and at a reasonable cost.

The Nature of Financial Reporting

A46   The preparation of financial statements involves judgment by management in applying the requirements of the entity's applicable financial reporting framework to the facts and circumstances of the entity. In addition, many financial statement items involve subjective decisions or assessments or a degree of uncertainty, and there may be a range of acceptable interpretations or judgments that may be made. Consequently, some financial statement items are subject to an inherent level of variability which cannot be eliminated by the application of additional auditing procedures. For example, this is often the case with respect to certain accounting estimates. Nevertheless, the ISAs (UK) require the auditor to give specific consideration to whether accounting estimates are reasonable in the context of the applicable financial reporting framework and related disclosures, and to the qualitative aspects of the entity's accounting practices, including indicators of possible bias in management's judgments.[20]

The Nature of Audit Procedures

A47   There are practical and legal limitations on the auditor's ability to obtain audit evidence. For example:

- There is the possibility that management or others may not provide, intentionally or unintentionally, the complete information that is relevant to the preparation of the financial statements or that has been requested by the auditor. Accordingly, the auditor cannot be certain of the completeness of information, even though the auditor has performed audit procedures to obtain assurance that all relevant information has been obtained.
- Fraud may involve sophisticated and carefully organized schemes designed to conceal it. Therefore, audit procedures used to gather audit evidence may be ineffective for detecting an intentional misstatement that involves, for example, collusion to falsify documentation which may cause the auditor to believe that audit evidence is valid when it is not. The auditor is neither trained as nor expected to be an expert in the authentication of documents.
- An audit is not an official investigation into alleged wrongdoing. Accordingly, the auditor is not given specific legal powers, such as the power of search, which may be necessary for such an investigation.

---

[20]   ISA (UK) 540 (Revised June 2016), Auditing Accounting Estimates, Including Fair Value Accounting Estimates, and Related Disclosures, and ISA (UK) 700 (Revised June 2016), Forming an Opinion and Reporting on Financial Statements, paragraph 13.

Timeliness of Financial Reporting and the Balance between Benefit and Cost

The matter of difficulty, time, or cost involved is not in itself a valid basis for the auditor **A48** to omit an audit procedure for which there is no alternative or to be satisfied with audit evidence that is less than persuasive. Appropriate planning assists in making sufficient time and resources available for the conduct of the audit. Notwithstanding this, the relevance of information, and thereby its value, tends to diminish over time, and there is a balance to be struck between the reliability of information and its cost. This is recognized in certain financial reporting frameworks (see, for example, the IASB's 'Framework for the Preparation and Presentation of Financial Statements'). Therefore, there is an expectation by users of financial statements that the auditor will form an opinion on the financial statements within a reasonable period of time and at a reasonable cost, recognizing that it is impracticable to address all information that may exist or to pursue every matter exhaustively on the assumption that information is in error or fraudulent until proved otherwise.

Consequently, it is necessary for the auditor to: **A49**

- Plan the audit so that it will be performed in an effective manner;
- Direct audit effort to areas most expected to contain risks of material misstatement, whether due to fraud or error, with correspondingly less effort directed at other areas; and
- Use testing and other means of examining populations for misstatements.

In light of the approaches described in paragraph A49, the ISAs (UK) contain requirements **A50** for the planning and performance of the audit and require the auditor, among other things, to:

- Have a basis for the identification and assessment of risks of material misstatement at the financial statement and assertion levels by performing risk assessment procedures and related activities;[21] and
- Use testing and other means of examining populations in a manner that provides a reasonable basis for the auditor to draw conclusions about the population.[22]

Other Matters that Affect the Inherent Limitations of an Audit

In the case of certain assertions or subject matters, the potential effects of the inherent **A51** limitations on the auditor's ability to detect material misstatements are particularly significant. Such assertions or subject matters include:

- Fraud, particularly fraud involving senior management or collusion. See ISA (UK) 240 (Revised June 2016) for further discussion.
- The existence and completeness of related party relationships and transactions. See ISA (UK) 550[23] for further discussion.
- The occurrence of non-compliance with laws and regulations. See ISA (UK) 250 (Revised June 2016)[24] for further discussion.
- Future events or conditions that may cause an entity to cease to continue as a going concern. See ISA (UK) 570 (Revised June 2016)[25] for further discussion.

---

[21] *ISA (UK) 315 (Revised June 2016), paragraphs 5–10.*

[22] *ISA (UK) 330 (Revised June 2016); ISA (UK) 500; ISA (UK) 520,* Analytical Procedures; *ISA (UK) 530,* Audit Sampling.

[23] *ISA (UK) 550,* Related Parties.

[24] *ISA (UK) 250 (Revised June 2016),* Consideration of Laws and Regulations in an Audit of Financial Statements.

[25] *ISA (UK) 570 (Revised June 2016),* Going Concern.

Relevant ISAs (UK) identify specific audit procedures to assist in mitigating the effect of the inherent limitations.

A52   Because of the inherent limitations of an audit, there is an unavoidable risk that some material misstatements of the financial statements may not be detected, even though the audit is properly planned and performed in accordance with ISAs (UK). Accordingly, the subsequent discovery of a material misstatement of the financial statements resulting from fraud or error does not by itself indicate a failure to conduct an audit in accordance with ISAs (UK). However, the inherent limitations of an audit are not a justification for the auditor to be satisfied with less-than-persuasive audit evidence. Whether the auditor has performed an audit in accordance with ISAs (UK) is determined by the audit procedures performed in the circumstances, the sufficiency and appropriateness of the audit evidence obtained as a result thereof and the suitability of the auditor's report based on an evaluation of that evidence in light of the overall objectives of the auditor.

Conduct of an Audit in Accordance with ISAs (UK)

Nature of the ISAs (UK) (Ref: Para. 18)

A53   The ISAs (UK), taken together, provide the standards for the auditor's work in fulfilling the overall objectives of the auditor. The ISAs (UK) deal with the general responsibilities of the auditor, as well as the auditor's further considerations relevant to the application of those responsibilities to specific topics.

A54   The scope, effective date and any specific limitation of the applicability of a specific ISA (UK) is made clear in the ISA (UK). Unless otherwise stated in the ISA (UK), the auditor is permitted to apply an ISA (UK) before the effective date specified therein.

A55   In performing an audit, the auditor may be required to comply with legal or regulatory requirements in addition to the ISAs (UK). The ISAs (UK) do not override law or regulation that governs an audit of financial statements. In the event that such law or regulation differs from the ISAs (UK), an audit conducted only in accordance with law or regulation will not automatically comply with ISAs (UK).

A56   The auditor may also conduct the audit in accordance with both ISAs (UK) and auditing standards of a specific jurisdiction or country. In such cases, in addition to complying with each of the ISAs (UK) relevant to the audit, it may be necessary for the auditor to perform additional audit procedures in order to comply with the relevant standards of that jurisdiction or country.

Considerations Specific to Audits in the Public Sector

A57   The ISAs (UK) are relevant to engagements in the public sector. The public sector auditor's responsibilities, however, may be affected by the audit mandate, or by obligations on public sector entities arising from law, regulation or other authority (such as ministerial directives, government policy requirements, or resolutions of the legislature), which may encompass a broader scope than an audit of financial statements in accordance with the ISAs (UK). These additional responsibilities are not dealt with in the ISAs (UK). They may be dealt with in the pronouncements of the International Organization of Supreme Audit Institutions or national standard setters, or in guidance developed by government audit agencies.

Contents of the ISAs (UK) (Ref: Para. 19)

In addition to objectives and requirements (requirements are expressed in the ISAs (UK) **A58** using 'shall'), an ISA (UK) contains related guidance in the form of application and other explanatory material. It may also contain introductory material that provides context relevant to a proper understanding of the ISA (UK), and definitions. The entire text of an ISA (UK), therefore, is relevant to an understanding of the objectives stated in an ISA (UK) and the proper application of the requirements of an ISA (UK).

Where necessary, the application and other explanatory material provides further **A59** explanation of the requirements of an ISA (UK) and guidance for carrying them out. In particular, it may:

- Explain more precisely what a requirement means or is intended to cover.
- Include examples of procedures that may be appropriate in the circumstances.

While such guidance does not in itself impose a requirement, it is relevant to the proper application of the requirements of an ISA (UK). The application and other explanatory material may also provide background information on matters addressed in an ISA (UK).

Appendices form part of the application and other explanatory material. The purpose and **A60** intended use of an appendix are explained in the body of the related ISA (UK) or within the title and introduction of the appendix itself.

Introductory material may include, as needed, such matters as explanation of: **A61**

- The purpose and scope of the ISA (UK), including how the ISA (UK) relates to other ISAs (UK).
- The subject matter of the ISA (UK).
- The respective responsibilities of the auditor and others in relation to the subject matter of the ISA (UK).
- The context in which the ISA (UK) is set.

An ISA (UK) may include, in a separate section under the heading 'Definitions,' a **A62** description of the meanings attributed to certain terms for purposes of the ISAs (UK). These are provided to assist in the consistent application and interpretation of the ISAs (UK), and are not intended to override definitions that may be established for other purposes, whether in law, regulation or otherwise. Unless otherwise indicated, those terms will carry the same meanings throughout the ISAs (UK). The Glossary of Terms relating to International Standards issued by the International Auditing and Assurance Standards Board in the *Handbook of International Quality Control, Auditing, Review, Other Assurance, and Related Services Pronouncements* published by IFAC contains a complete listing of terms defined in the ISAs (UK). It also includes descriptions of other terms found in ISAs (UK) to assist in common and consistent interpretation and translation.

When appropriate, additional considerations specific to audits of smaller entities and **A63** public sector entities are included within the application and other explanatory material of an ISA (UK). These additional considerations assist in the application of the requirements of the ISA (UK) in the audit of such entities. They do not, however, limit or reduce the responsibility of the auditor to apply and comply with the requirements of the ISAs (UK).

Considerations Specific to Smaller Entities

For purposes of specifying additional considerations to audits of smaller entities, a 'smaller **A64** entity' refers to an entity which typically possesses qualitative characteristics such as:

(a) Concentration of ownership and management in a small number of individuals (often a single individual – either a natural person or another enterprise that owns the entity provided the owner exhibits the relevant qualitative characteristics); and

(b) One or more of the following:

    (i)   Straightforward or uncomplicated transactions;

    (ii)   Simple record-keeping;

    (iii) Few lines of business and few products within business lines;

    (iv) Few internal controls;

    (v)   Few levels of management with responsibility for a broad range of controls; or

    (vi) Few personnel, many having a wide range of duties.

These qualitative characteristics are not exhaustive, they are not exclusive to smaller entities, and smaller entities do not necessarily display all of these characteristics.

A65   The considerations specific to smaller entities included in the ISAs (UK) have been developed primarily with unlisted entities in mind. Some of the considerations, however, may be helpful in audits of smaller listed entities.

A66   The ISAs (UK) refer to the proprietor of a smaller entity who is involved in running the entity on a day-to-day basis as the 'owner-manager.'

Objectives Stated in Individual ISAs (UK) (Ref: Para. 21)

A67   Each ISA (UK) contains one or more objectives which provide a link between the requirements and the overall objectives of the auditor. The objectives in individual ISAs (UK) serve to focus the auditor on the desired outcome of the ISA (UK), while being specific enough to assist the auditor in:

- Understanding what needs to be accomplished and, where necessary, the appropriate means of doing so; and

- Deciding whether more needs to be done to achieve them in the particular circumstances of the audit.

A68   Objectives are to be understood in the context of the overall objectives of the auditor stated in paragraph 11 of this ISA (UK). As with the overall objectives of the auditor, the ability to achieve an individual objective is equally subject to the inherent limitations of an audit.

A69   In using the objectives, the auditor is required to have regard to the interrelationships among the ISAs (UK). This is because, as indicated in paragraph A53, the ISAs (UK) deal in some cases with general responsibilities and in others with the application of those responsibilities to specific topics. For example, this ISA (UK) requires the auditor to adopt an attitude of professional skepticism; this is necessary in all aspects of planning and performing an audit but is not repeated as a requirement of each ISA (UK). At a more detailed level, ISA (UK) 315 (Revised June 2016) and ISA (UK) 330 (Revised June 2016) contain, among other things, objectives and requirements that deal with the auditor's responsibilities to identify and assess the risks of material misstatement and to design and perform further audit procedures to respond to those assessed risks, respectively; these objectives and requirements apply throughout the audit. An ISA (UK) dealing with specific aspects of the audit (for example, ISA (UK) 540 (Revised June 2016)) may expand on how the objectives and requirements of such ISAs (UK) as ISA (UK) 315 (Revised June 2016) and ISA (UK) 330 (Revised June 2016) are to be applied in relation to the subject of the ISA (UK) but does not repeat them. Thus, in achieving the objective stated in ISA (UK) 540 (Revised June 2016), the auditor has regard to the objectives and requirements of other relevant ISAs (UK).

Use of Objectives to Determine Need for Additional Audit Procedures (Ref: Para. 21(a))

The requirements of the ISAs (UK) are designed to enable the auditor to achieve the   **A70**
objectives specified in the ISAs (UK), and thereby the overall objectives of the auditor. The
proper application of the requirements of the ISAs (UK) by the auditor is therefore expected
to provide a sufficient basis for the auditor's achievement of the objectives. However,
because the circumstances of audit engagements vary widely and all such circumstances
cannot be anticipated in the ISAs (UK), the auditor is responsible for determining the
audit procedures necessary to fulfill the requirements of the ISAs (UK) and to achieve the
objectives. In the circumstances of an engagement, there may be particular matters that
require the auditor to perform audit procedures in addition to those required by the ISAs
(UK) to meet the objectives specified in the ISAs (UK).

*Use of Objectives to Evaluate Whether Sufficient Appropriate Audit Evidence Has Been
Obtained* (Ref: Para. 21(b))

The auditor is required to use the objectives to evaluate whether sufficient appropriate   **A71**
audit evidence has been obtained in the context of the overall objectives of the auditor. If
as a result the auditor concludes that the audit evidence is not sufficient and appropriate,
then the auditor may follow one or more of the following approaches to meeting the
requirement of paragraph 21(b):

- Evaluate whether further relevant audit evidence has been, or will be, obtained as a
  result of complying with other ISAs (UK);
- Extend the work performed in applying one or more requirements; or
- Perform other procedures judged by the auditor to be necessary in the circumstances.

Where none of the above is expected to be practical or possible in the circumstances, the
auditor will not be able to obtain sufficient appropriate audit evidence and is required by
the ISAs (UK) to determine the effect on the auditor's report or on the auditor's ability to
complete the engagement.

Complying with Relevant Requirements

Relevant Requirements (Ref: Para. 22)

In some cases, an ISA (UK) (and therefore all of its requirements) may not be relevant   **A72**
in the circumstances. For example, if an entity does not have an internal audit function,
nothing in ISA (UK) 610 (Revised June 2013)[26] is relevant.

Within a relevant ISA (UK), there may be conditional requirements. Such a requirement   **A73**
is relevant when the circumstances envisioned in the requirement apply and the condition
exists. In general, the conditionality of a requirement will either be explicit or implicit, for
example:

- The requirement to modify the auditor's opinion if there is a limitation of scope[27]
  represents an explicit conditional requirement.

---

[26] *ISA (UK) 610 (Revised June 2013)*, Using the Work of Internal Auditors, *Paragraph 2.*

[27] *ISA (UK) 705 (Revised June 2016)*, Modifications to the Opinion in the Independent Auditor's Report,
paragraph 13.

- The requirement to communicate significant deficiencies in internal control identified during the audit to those charged with governance,[28] which depends on the existence of such identified significant deficiencies; and the requirement to obtain sufficient appropriate audit evidence regarding the presentation and disclosure of segment information in accordance with the applicable financial reporting framework,[29] which depends on that framework requiring or permitting such disclosure, represent implicit conditional requirements.

In some cases, a requirement may be expressed as being conditional on applicable law or regulation. For example, the auditor may be required to withdraw from the audit engagement, *where withdrawal is possible under applicable law or regulation*, or the auditor may be required to do something, *unless prohibited by law or regulation*. Depending on the jurisdiction, the legal or regulatory permission or prohibition may be explicit or implicit.

Departure from a Requirement (Ref: Para. 23)

A74   ISA (UK) 230 (Revised June 2016) establishes documentation requirements in those exceptional circumstances where the auditor departs from a relevant requirement.[30] The ISAs (UK) do not call for compliance with a requirement that is not relevant in the circumstances of the audit.

Failure to Achieve an Objective (Ref: Para. 24)

A75   Whether an objective has been achieved is a matter for the auditor's professional judgment. That judgment takes account of the results of audit procedures performed in complying with the requirements of the ISAs (UK), and the auditor's evaluation of whether sufficient appropriate audit evidence has been obtained and whether more needs to be done in the particular circumstances of the audit to achieve the objectives stated in the ISAs (UK). Accordingly, circumstances that may give rise to a failure to achieve an objective include those that:

- Prevent the auditor from complying with the relevant requirements of an ISA (UK).
- Result in its not being practicable or possible for the auditor to carry out the additional audit procedures or obtain further audit evidence as determined necessary from the use of the objectives in accordance with paragraph 21, for example due to a limitation in the available audit evidence.

A76   Audit documentation that meets the requirements of ISA (UK) 230 (Revised June 2016) and the specific documentation requirements of other relevant ISAs (UK) provides evidence of the auditor's basis for a conclusion about the achievement of the overall objectives of the auditor. While it is unnecessary for the auditor to document separately (as in a checklist, for example) that individual objectives have been achieved, the documentation of a failure to achieve an objective assists the auditor's evaluation of whether such a failure has prevented the auditor from achieving the overall objectives of the auditor.

---

[28] *ISA (UK) 265*, Communicating Deficiencies in Internal Control to Those Charged with Governance and Management, *paragraph 9.*

[29] *ISA (UK) 501*, Audit Evidence—Specific Considerations for Selected Items, *paragraph 13.*

[30] *ISA (UK) 230 (Revised June 2016), paragraph 12.*

International Standard on Auditing (UK) 210 (Revised June 2016)

Agreeing the terms of audit engagements

(Effective for audits of financial statements for periods commencing on or after 17 June 2016)

Contents

International Standard on Auditing (UK) (ISA (UK)) 210 (Revised June 2016), *Agreeing the Terms of Audit Engagements* should be read in conjunction with ISA (UK) 200 (Revised June 2016), *Overall Objectives of the Independent Auditor and the Conduct of an Audit in Accordance with International Standards on Auditing (UK)*.

Introduction

Scope of this ISA (UK)

1   This International Standard on Auditing (UK) (ISA (UK)) deals with the auditor's responsibilities in agreeing the terms of the audit engagement with management and, where appropriate, those charged with governance. This includes establishing that certain preconditions for an audit, responsibility for which rests with management and, where appropriate, those charged with governance, are present. ISA (UK) 220 (Revised June 2016)[1] deals with those aspects of engagement acceptance that are within the control of the auditor. (Ref: Para. A1)

Effective Date

2   This ISA (UK) is effective for audits of financial statements for periods commencing on or after 17 June 2016. Earlier adoption is permitted.

Objective

3   The objective of the auditor is to accept or continue an audit engagement only when the basis upon which it is to be performed has been agreed, through:

(a)   Establishing whether the preconditions for an audit are present; and

(b)   Confirming that there is a common understanding between the auditor and management and, where appropriate, those charged with governance of the terms of the audit engagement.

Definitions

4   For purposes of the ISAs (UK), the following term has the meaning attributed below:

Preconditions for an audit – The use by management[1a] of an acceptable financial reporting framework in the preparation of the financial statements and the agreement of management and, where appropriate, those charged with governance to the premise[2] on which an audit is conducted.

5   For the purposes of this ISA (UK), references to 'management' should be read hereafter as 'management and, where appropriate, those charged with governance.'

Requirements

Preconditions for an Audit

6   In order to establish whether the preconditions for an audit are present, the auditor shall:

(a)   Determine whether the financial reporting framework to be applied in the preparation of the financial statements is acceptable; and (Ref: Para. A2–A10)

(b)   Obtain the agreement of management that it acknowledges and understands its responsibility: (Ref: Para. A11–A14, A21)

---

[1]   *ISA (UK) 220 (Revised June 2016)*, Quality Control for an Audit of Financial Statements.

[1a]   In the UK those charged with governance are responsible for the preparation of the financial statements.

[2]   *ISA (UK) 200 (Revised June 2016)*, Overall Objectives of the Independent Auditor and the Conduct of an Audit in Accordance with International Standards on Auditing (UK), *paragraph 13*.

(i)   For the preparation of the financial statements in accordance with the applicable financial reporting framework, including where relevant their fair presentation; (Ref: Para. A15–A15-2)

(ii) For such internal control as management determines is necessary to enable the preparation of financial statements that are free from material misstatement, whether due to fraud or error; and (Ref: Para. A16–A19)

(iii) To provide the auditor with:[2a]

    (a)   Access to all information of which management is aware that is relevant to the preparation of the financial statements such as records, documentation and other matters;

    (b)   Additional information that the auditor may request from management for the purpose of the audit; and

    (c)   Unrestricted access to persons within the entity from whom the auditor determines it necessary to obtain audit evidence.

Limitation on Scope Prior to Audit Engagement Acceptance

If management or those charged with governance impose a limitation on the scope of the auditor's work in the terms of a proposed audit engagement such that the auditor believes the limitation will result in the auditor disclaiming an opinion on the financial statements, the auditor shall not accept such a limited engagement as an audit engagement, unless required by law or regulation to do so.   **7**

Other Factors Affecting Audit Engagement Acceptance

If the preconditions for an audit are not present, the auditor shall discuss the matter with management. Unless required by law or regulation to do so, the auditor shall not accept the proposed audit engagement: **8**

(a)   If the auditor has determined that the financial reporting framework to be applied in the preparation of the financial statements is unacceptable, except as provided in paragraph 19; or

(b)   If the agreement referred to in paragraph 6(b) has not been obtained.

Agreement on Audit Engagement Terms

The auditor shall agree the terms of the audit engagement with management or those charged with governance, as appropriate. (Ref: Para. A22)   **9**

Subject to paragraph 11, the agreed terms of the audit engagement shall be recorded in an audit engagement letter or other suitable form of written agreement and shall include: (Ref: Para. A23–A27)   **10**

(a)   The objective and scope of the audit of the financial statements;

(b)   The responsibilities of the auditor;

(c)   The responsibilities of management;[2b]

(d)   Identification of the applicable financial reporting framework for the preparation of the financial statements; and

(e)   Reference to the expected form and content of any reports to be issued by the auditor; and (Ref: Para. A23a)

[2a] Sections 499 and 500 of the Companies Act 2006 set legal requirements in relation to the auditor's right to obtain information.

[2b] In the UK, the engagement letter sets out the responsibilities of those charged with governance.

(f)   A statement that there may be circumstances in which a report may differ from its expected form and content.

11   If law or regulation prescribes in sufficient detail the terms of the audit engagement referred to in paragraph 10, the auditor need not record them in a written agreement, except for the fact that such law or regulation applies and that management acknowledges and understands its responsibilities as set out in paragraph 6(b). (Ref: Para. A22, A26–A27)

12   If law or regulation prescribes responsibilities of management similar to those described in paragraph 6(b), the auditor may determine that the law or regulation includes responsibilities that, in the auditor's judgment, are equivalent in effect to those set out in that paragraph. For such responsibilities that are equivalent, the auditor may use the wording of the law or regulation to describe them in the written agreement. For those responsibilities that are not prescribed by law or regulation such that their effect is equivalent, the written agreement shall use the description in paragraph 6(b). (Ref: Para. A26)

Recurring Audits

13   On recurring audits, the auditor shall assess whether circumstances require the terms of the audit engagement to be revised and whether there is a need to remind the entity of the existing terms of the audit engagement. (Ref: Para. A28)

Acceptance of a Change in the Terms of the Audit Engagement

14   The auditor shall not agree to a change in the terms of the audit engagement where there is no reasonable justification for doing so. (Ref: Para. A29–A31)

15   If, prior to completing the audit engagement, the auditor is requested to change the audit engagement to an engagement that conveys a lower level of assurance, the auditor shall determine whether there is reasonable justification for doing so. (Ref: Para. A32–A33)

16   If the terms of the audit engagement are changed, the auditor and management shall agree on and record the new terms of the engagement in an engagement letter or other suitable form of written agreement.

17   If the auditor is unable to agree to a change of the terms of the audit engagement and is not permitted by management to continue the original audit engagement, the auditor shall:

(a)   Withdraw from the audit engagement where possible under applicable law or regulation; and

(b)   Determine whether there is any obligation, either contractual or otherwise, to report the circumstances to other parties, such as those charged with governance, owners or regulators. (Ref: Para. A33-1)

Additional Considerations in Engagement Acceptance

Financial Reporting Standards Supplemented by Law or Regulation

18   If financial reporting standards established by an authorized or recognized standards setting organization are supplemented by law or regulation, the auditor shall determine whether there are any conflicts between the financial reporting standards and the additional

requirements. If such conflicts exist, the auditor shall discuss with management the nature of the additional requirements and shall agree whether:

(a)   The additional requirements can be met through additional disclosures in the financial statements; or

(b)   The description of the applicable financial reporting framework in the financial statements can be amended accordingly.

If neither of the above actions is possible, the auditor shall determine whether it will be necessary to modify the auditor's opinion in accordance with ISA (UK) 705 (Revised June 2016).[3] (Ref: Para. A34)

Financial Reporting Framework Prescribed by Law or Regulation—Other Matters Affecting Acceptance

If the auditor has determined that the financial reporting framework prescribed by law or   **19** regulation would be unacceptable but for the fact that it is prescribed by law or regulation, the auditor shall accept the audit engagement only if the following conditions are present: (Ref: Para. A35)

(a)   Management agrees to provide additional disclosures in the financial statements required to avoid the financial statements being misleading; and

(b)   It is recognized in the terms of the audit engagement that:

   (i)   The auditor's report on the financial statements will incorporate an Emphasis of Matter paragraph, drawing users' attention to the additional disclosures, in accordance with ISA (UK) 706 (Revised June 2016);[4] and

   (ii)   Unless the auditor is required by law or regulation to express the auditor's opinion on the financial statements by using the phrases 'present fairly, in all material respects,' or 'give a true and fair view' in accordance with the applicable financial reporting framework, the auditor's opinion on the financial statements will not include such phrases.

If the conditions outlined in paragraph 19 are not present and the auditor is required by law   **20** or regulation to undertake the audit engagement, the auditor shall:

(a)   Evaluate the effect of the misleading nature of the financial statements on the auditor's report; and

(b)   Include appropriate reference to this matter in the terms of the audit engagement.

Auditor's Report Prescribed by Law or Regulation

In some cases, law or regulation of the relevant jurisdiction prescribes the layout or   **21** wording of the auditor's report in a form or in terms that are significantly different from the requirements of ISAs (UK). In these circumstances, the auditor shall evaluate:

(a)   Whether users might misunderstand the assurance obtained from the audit of the financial statements and, if so,

(b)   Whether additional explanation in the auditor's report can mitigate possible misunderstanding.[5]

---

[3] *ISA (UK) 705 (Revised June 2016)*, Modifications to the Opinion in the Independent Auditor's Report.

[4] *ISA (UK) 706 (Revised June 2016)*, Emphasis of Matter Paragraphs and Other Matter Paragraphs in the Independent Auditor's Report.

[5] *ISA (UK) 706 (Revised June 2016)*.

If the auditor concludes that additional explanation in the auditor's report cannot mitigate possible misunderstanding, the auditor shall not accept the audit engagement, unless required by law or regulation to do so. An audit conducted in accordance with such law or regulation does not comply with ISAs (UK). Accordingly, the auditor shall not include any reference within the auditor's report to the audit having been conducted in accordance with ISAs (UK).[6] (Ref: Para. A36–A37)

***

Application and Other Explanatory Material

Scope of this ISA (UK) (Ref: Para. 1)

A1   Assurance engagements, which include audit engagements, may only be accepted when the practitioner considers that relevant ethical requirements such as independence and professional competence will be satisfied, and when the engagement exhibits certain characteristics.[7] The auditor's responsibilities in respect of ethical requirements in the context of the acceptance of an audit engagement and in so far as they are within the control of the auditor are dealt with in ISA (UK) 220 (Revised June 2016).[8] This ISA (UK) deals with those matters (or preconditions) that are within the control of the entity and upon which it is necessary for the auditor and the entity's management to agree.

Preconditions for an Audit

The Financial Reporting Framework (Ref: Para. 6(a))

A2   A condition for acceptance of an assurance engagement is that the criteria referred to in the definition of an assurance engagement are suitable and available to intended users.[9] Criteria are the benchmarks used to evaluate or measure the subject matter including, where relevant, benchmarks for presentation and disclosure. Suitable criteria enable reasonably consistent evaluation or measurement of a subject matter within the context of professional judgment. For purposes of the ISAs (UK), the applicable financial reporting framework provides the criteria the auditor uses to audit the financial statements, including where relevant their fair presentation.

A3   Without an acceptable financial reporting framework, management does not have an appropriate basis for the preparation of the financial statements and the auditor does not have suitable criteria for auditing the financial statements. In many cases the auditor may presume that the applicable financial reporting framework is acceptable, as described in paragraphs A8–A9.

---

[6] *See also ISA (UK) 700 (Revised June 2016)*, Forming an Opinion and Reporting on Financial Statements, *paragraph 43.*

[7] International Framework for Assurance Engagements, *paragraph 17.*
The International Framework for Assurance Engagements has not been promulgated by the FRC for application in the UK.

[8] *ISA (UK) 220 (Revised June 2016), paragraphs 9–11.*

[9] International Framework for Assurance Engagements, *paragraph 17(b)(ii).*
The International Framework for Assurance Engagements has not been promulgated by the FRC for application in the UK.

Determining the Acceptability of the Financial Reporting Framework

Factors that are relevant to the auditor's determination of the acceptability of the financial   **A4**
reporting framework to be applied in the preparation of the financial statements include:

- The nature of the entity (for example, whether it is a business enterprise, a public sector entity or a not for profit organization);
- The purpose of the financial statements (for example, whether they are prepared to meet the common financial information needs of a wide range of users or the financial information needs of specific users);
- The nature of the financial statements (for example, whether the financial statements are a complete set of financial statements or a single financial statement); and
- Whether law or regulation prescribes the applicable financial reporting framework.

Many users of financial statements are not in a position to demand financial statements   **A5**
tailored to meet their specific information needs. While all the information needs of
specific users cannot be met, there are financial information needs that are common to a
wide range of users. Financial statements prepared in accordance with a financial reporting
framework designed to meet the common financial information needs of a wide range of
users are referred to as general purpose financial statements.

In some cases, the financial statements will be prepared in accordance with a financial   **A6**
reporting framework designed to meet the financial information needs of specific users.
Such financial statements are referred to as special purpose financial statements. The
financial information needs of the intended users will determine the applicable financial
reporting framework in these circumstances. ISA 800 discusses the acceptability of
financial reporting frameworks designed to meet the financial information needs of
specific users.[10]

Deficiencies in the applicable financial reporting framework that indicate that the   **A7**
framework is not acceptable may be encountered after the audit engagement has been
accepted. When use of that framework is prescribed by law or regulation, the requirements
of paragraphs 19–20 apply. When use of that framework is not prescribed by law or
regulation, management may decide to adopt another framework that is acceptable. When
management does so, as required by paragraph 16, new terms of the audit engagement
are agreed to reflect the change in the framework as the previously agreed terms will no
longer be accurate.

General purpose frameworks

At present, there is no objective and authoritative basis that has been generally recognized   **A8**
globally for judging the acceptability of general purpose frameworks. In the absence of such
a basis, financial reporting standards established by organizations that are authorized or
recognized to promulgate standards to be used by certain types of entities are presumed to
be acceptable for general purpose financial statements prepared by such entities, provided
the organizations follow an established and transparent process involving deliberation and
consideration of the views of a wide range of stakeholders. Examples of such financial
reporting standards include:

- International Financial Reporting Standards (IFRSs) promulgated by the International Accounting Standards Board;

---

[10] *ISA 800,* Special Considerations—Audits of Financial Statements Prepared in Accordance with Special Purpose Frameworks, *paragraph 8.*
ISA 800 has not been promulgated by the FRC for application in the UK.

- International Public Sector Accounting Standards (IPSASs) promulgated by the International Public Sector Accounting Standards Board; and
- Accounting principles promulgated by an authorized or recognized standards setting organization in a particular jurisdiction, provided the organization follows an established and transparent process involving deliberation and consideration of the views of a wide range of stakeholders.

These financial reporting standards are often identified as the applicable financial reporting framework in law or regulation governing the preparation of general purpose financial statements.

Financial reporting frameworks prescribed by law or regulation

A9   In accordance with paragraph 6(a), the auditor is required to determine whether the financial reporting framework, to be applied in the preparation of the financial statements, is acceptable. In some jurisdictions, law or regulation may prescribe the financial reporting framework to be used in the preparation of general purpose financial statements for certain types of entities. In the absence of indications to the contrary, such a financial reporting framework is presumed to be acceptable for general purpose financial statements prepared by such entities. In the event that the framework is not considered to be acceptable, paragraphs 19–20 apply.

Jurisdictions that do not have standards setting organizations or prescribed financial reporting frameworks

A10   When an entity is registered or operating in a jurisdiction that does not have an authorized or recognized standards setting organization, or where use of the financial reporting framework is not prescribed by law or regulation, management identifies a financial reporting framework to be applied in the preparation of the financial statements. Appendix 2 contains guidance on determining the acceptability of financial reporting frameworks in such circumstances.

Agreement of the Responsibilities of Management (Ref: Para. 6(b))

A11   An audit in accordance with ISAs (UK) is conducted on the premise that management has acknowledged and understands that it has the responsibilities set out in paragraph 6(b).[11] In certain jurisdictions, such responsibilities may be specified in law or regulation. In others, there may be little or no legal or regulatory definition of such responsibilities. ISAs (UK) do not override law or regulation in such matters. However, the concept of an independent audit requires that the auditor's role does not involve taking responsibility for the preparation of the financial statements or for the entity's related internal control, and that the auditor has a reasonable expectation of obtaining the information necessary for the audit (including information obtained from outside of the general and subsidiary ledgers) in so far as management is able to provide or procure it. Accordingly, the premise is fundamental to the conduct of an independent audit. To avoid misunderstanding, agreement is reached with management that it acknowledges and understands that it has such responsibilities as part of agreeing and recording the terms of the audit engagement in paragraphs 9–12.

A12   The way in which the responsibilities for financial reporting are divided between management and those charged with governance will vary according to the resources and structure of the entity and any relevant law or regulation, and the respective roles

---

[11] *ISA (UK) 200 (Revised June 2016), paragraph A2.*

of management and those charged with governance within the entity. In most cases, management is responsible for execution while those charged with governance have oversight of management. In some cases, those charged with governance will have, or will assume, responsibility for approving the financial statements or monitoring the entity's internal control related to financial reporting. In larger or public entities, a subgroup of those charged with governance, such as an audit committee, may be charged with certain oversight responsibilities.

ISA (UK) 580 requires the auditor to request management to provide written representations   **A13**
that it has fulfilled certain of its responsibilities.[12] It may therefore be appropriate to make management aware that receipt of such written representations will be expected, together with written representations required by other ISAs (UK) and, where necessary, written representations to support other audit evidence relevant to the financial statements or one or more specific assertions in the financial statements.

Where management will not acknowledge its responsibilities, or agree to provide the   **A14**
written representations, the auditor will be unable to obtain sufficient appropriate audit evidence.[13] In such circumstances, it would not be appropriate for the auditor to accept the audit engagement, unless law or regulation requires the auditor to do so. In cases where the auditor is required to accept the audit engagement, the auditor may need to explain to management the importance of these matters, and the implications for the auditor's report.

Preparation of the Financial Statements (Ref: Para. 6(b)(i))

Most financial reporting frameworks include requirements relating to the presentation of   **A15**
the financial statements; for such frameworks, *preparation* of the financial statements in accordance with the financial reporting framework includes *presentation*. In the case of a fair presentation framework the importance of the reporting objective of fair presentation is such that the premise agreed with management includes specific reference to fair presentation, or to the responsibility to ensure that the financial statements will 'give a true and fair view' in accordance with the financial reporting framework.

In the UK, accounting standards relating to the small companies regime are prohibited   **A15-1**
by EU law from specifying disclosure requirements in addition to the limited number of disclosures set out in the Accounting Directive, even though the financial statements of those small entities are required by law to give a true and fair view.[13a] Further, it is not sufficient for the auditor to conclude that the financial statements give a true and fair view solely on the basis that the financial statements were prepared in accordance with accounting standards and any other applicable legal requirements.[13b] The auditor therefore considers whether additional disclosures will be necessary in the financial statements when compliance with an accounting standard is insufficient to give a true and fair view.

Where the auditor determines that the financial statements do not provide the   **A15-2**
additional disclosures necessary to achieve fair presentation, ISA (UK) 450 (Revised

---

[12] *ISA (UK) 580, Written Representations, paragraphs 10–11.*

[13] *ISA (UK) 580, paragraph A26.*

[13a] *In the United Kingdom, the Companies Act 2006 establishes this requirement.*

[13b] *ISA (UK) 700 (Revised June 2016), paragraph 16.*

June 2016)[13c] and ISA (UK) 700 (Revised June 2016)[13d] establish requirements and provide guidance on the evaluation and disposition of misstatements and the effect on the auditor's opinion in the auditor's report.

Internal Control (Ref: Para. 6(b)(ii))

A16   Management maintains such internal control as it determines is necessary to enable the preparation of financial statements that are free from material misstatement, whether due to fraud or error. Internal control, no matter how effective, can provide an entity with only reasonable assurance about achieving the entity's financial reporting objectives due to the inherent limitations of internal control.[14]

A17   An independent audit conducted in accordance with the ISAs (UK) does not act as a substitute for the maintenance of internal control necessary for the preparation of financial statements by management. Accordingly, the auditor is required to obtain the agreement of management that it acknowledges and understands its responsibility for internal control. However, the agreement required by paragraph 6(b)(ii) does not imply that the auditor will find that internal control maintained by management has achieved its purpose or will be free of deficiencies.

A18   It is for management to determine what internal control is necessary to enable the preparation of the financial statements. The term 'internal control' encompasses a wide range of activities within components that may be described as the control environment; the entity's risk assessment process; the information system, including the related business processes relevant to financial reporting, and communication; control activities; and monitoring of controls. This division, however, does not necessarily reflect how a particular entity may design, implement and maintain its internal control, or how it may classify any particular component.[15] An entity's internal control (in particular, its accounting books and records, or accounting systems) will reflect the needs of management, the complexity of the business, the nature of the risks to which the entity is subject, and relevant laws or regulation.

A19   In some jurisdictions, law or regulation may refer to the responsibility of management for the adequacy of accounting books and records, or accounting systems. In some cases, general practice may assume a distinction between accounting books and records or accounting systems on the one hand, and internal control or controls on the other. As accounting books and records, or accounting systems, are an integral part of internal control as referred to in paragraph A18, no specific reference is made to them in paragraph 6(b)(ii) for the description of the responsibility of management. To avoid misunderstanding, it may be appropriate for the auditor to explain to management the scope of this responsibility.

Additional Information (Ref: Para. 6(b)(iii)b)

A19a   Additional information that the auditor may request from management for the purpose of the audit may include when applicable, matters related to other information in accordance with ISA (UK) 720 (Revised June 2016). When the auditor expects to obtain other information after the date of the auditor's report, the terms of the audit engagement

---

[13c] *ISA (UK) 450 (Revised June 2016),* Evaluation of Misstatements Identified During the Audit.

[13d] *ISA (UK) 700 (Revised June 2016).*

[14] *ISA (UK) 315 (Revised June 2016),* Identifying and Assessing the Risks of Material Misstatement through Understanding the Entity and Its Environment, *paragraph A46.*

[15] *ISA (UK) 315 (Revised June 2016), paragraph A51 and Appendix 1.*

may also acknowledge the auditor's responsibilities relating to such other information including, if applicable, the actions that may be appropriate or necessary if the auditor concludes that a material misstatement of the other information exists in other information obtained after the date of the auditor's report.[15a]

Considerations Relevant to Smaller Entities (Ref: Para. 6(b))

One of the purposes of agreeing the terms of the audit engagement is to avoid misunderstanding about the respective responsibilities of management and the auditor. For example, when a third party has assisted with the preparation of the financial statements, it may be useful to remind management that the preparation of the financial statements in accordance with the applicable financial reporting framework remains its responsibility.   **A20**

Agreement on Audit Engagement Terms

Agreeing the Terms of the Audit Engagement (Ref: Para. 9)

The roles of management and those charged with governance in agreeing the terms of the audit engagement for the entity depend on the governance structure of the entity and relevant law or regulation.   **A21**

Audit Engagement Letter or Other Form of Written Agreement[16] (Ref: Para. 10–11)

It is in the interests of both the entity and the auditor that the auditor sends an audit engagement letter before the commencement of the audit to help avoid misunderstandings with respect to the audit. In some countries, however, the objective and scope of an audit and the responsibilities of management and of the auditor may be sufficiently established by law, that is, they prescribe the matters described in paragraph 10. Although in these circumstances paragraph 11 permits the auditor to include in the engagement letter only reference to the fact that relevant law or regulation applies and that management acknowledges and understands its responsibilities as set out in paragraph 6(b), the auditor may nevertheless consider it appropriate to include the matters described in paragraph 10 in an engagement letter for the information of management.   **A22**

Form and Content of the Audit Engagement Letter

The form and content of the audit engagement letter may vary for each entity. Information included in the audit engagement letter on the auditor's responsibilities may be based on ISA (UK) 200 (Revised June 2016).[17] Paragraphs 6(b) and 12 of this ISA (UK) deal with the description of the responsibilities of management. In addition to including the matters required by paragraph 10, an audit engagement letter may make reference to, for example: **A23**

- Elaboration of the scope of the audit, including reference to applicable legislation, regulations, ISAs (UK), and ethical and other pronouncements of professional bodies to which the auditor adheres.

[15a] *ISA (UK) 700 (Revised June 2016) requires that 'The auditor shall not sign, and hence date, the auditor's report earlier than the date on which all the other information contained in the annual report has been approved by those charged with governance and the auditor has considered all necessary available evidence.'*

[16] *In the paragraphs that follow, any reference to an audit engagement letter is to be taken as a reference to an audit engagement letter or other suitable form of written agreement.*

[17] *ISA (UK) 200 (Revised June 2016), paragraphs 3–9.*

- The form of any other communication of results of the audit engagement.
- The requirement for the auditor to communicate key audit matters in the auditor's report in accordance with ISA (UK) 701.[18]
- The fact that because of the inherent limitations of an audit, together with the inherent limitations of internal control, there is an unavoidable risk that some material misstatements may not be detected, even though the audit is properly planned and performed in accordance with ISAs (UK).
- Arrangements regarding the planning and performance of the audit, including the composition of the audit team.
- The expectation that management will provide written representations (see also paragraph A13).
- The expectation that management will provide access to all information of which management is aware that is relevant to the preparation of the financial statements, including an expectation that management will provide access to information relevant to disclosures.
- The agreement of management to make available to the auditor draft financial statements, including all information relevant to their preparation, whether obtained from within or outside of the general and subsidiary ledgers (including all information relevant to the preparation of disclosures), and the other information,[19] if any, in time to allow the auditor to complete the audit in accordance with the proposed timetable.
- The agreement of management to inform the auditor of facts that may affect the financial statements, of which management may become aware during the period from the date of the auditor's report to the date the financial statements are issued.
- The basis on which fees are computed and any billing arrangements.
- A request for management to acknowledge receipt of the audit engagement letter and to agree to the terms of the engagement outlined therein.

A23a   When the auditor is not required to communicate key audit matters, it may be helpful for the auditor to make reference in the terms of the audit engagement to the possibility of communicating key audit matters in the auditor's report and, in certain jurisdictions, it may be necessary for the auditor to include a reference to such possibility in order to retain the ability to do so.

A24   When relevant, the following points could also be made in the audit engagement letter:

- Arrangements concerning the involvement of other auditors and experts in some aspects of the audit.
- Arrangements concerning the involvement of internal auditors and other staff of the entity.
- Arrangements to be made with the predecessor auditor, if any, in the case of an initial audit.
- Any restriction of the auditor's liability when such possibility exists.
- A reference to any further agreements between the auditor and the entity.
- Any obligations to provide audit working papers to other parties.

An example of an audit engagement letter is set out in Appendix 1.[19a]

---

[18] *ISA (UK) 701*, Communicating Key Audit Matters in the Independent Auditor's Report.

[19] *As defined in ISA (UK) 720 (Revised June 2016)*, The Auditor's Responsibilities Relating to Other Information.

[19a] *The example letter in Appendix 1 has not been tailored for the UK.*

Audits of Components

When the auditor of a parent entity is also the auditor of a component, the factors that may   **A25**
influence the decision whether to send a separate audit engagement letter to the component
include the following:

* Who appoints the component auditor;
* Whether a separate auditor's report is to be issued on the component;
* Legal requirements in relation to audit appointments;
* Degree of ownership by parent; and
* Degree of independence of the component management from the parent entity.

Responsibilities of Management Prescribed by Law or Regulation (Ref: Para. 11–12)

If, in the circumstances described in paragraphs A22 and A27, the auditor concludes that   **A26**
it is not necessary to record certain terms of the audit engagement in an audit engagement
letter, the auditor is still required by paragraph 11 to seek the written agreement from
management that it acknowledges and understands that it has the responsibilities set out in
paragraph 6(b). However, in accordance with paragraph 12, such written agreement may
use the wording of the law or regulation if such law or regulation establishes responsibilities
for management that are equivalent in effect to those described in paragraph 6(b). The
accounting profession, audit standards setter, or audit regulator in a jurisdiction may have
provided guidance as to whether the description in law or regulation is equivalent.

Considerations specific to public sector entities

Law or regulation governing the operations of public sector audits generally mandate   **A27**
the appointment of a public sector auditor and commonly set out the public sector
auditor's responsibilities and powers, including the power to access an entity's records
and other information. When law or regulation prescribes in sufficient detail the terms of
the audit engagement, the public sector auditor may nonetheless consider that there are
benefits in issuing a fuller audit engagement letter than permitted by paragraph 11.

Recurring Audits (Ref: Para. 13)

The auditor may decide not to send a new audit engagement letter or other written   **A28**
agreement each period. However, the following factors may make it appropriate to revise
the terms of the audit engagement or to remind the entity of existing terms:

* Any indication that the entity misunderstands the objective and scope of the audit.
* Any revised or special terms of the audit engagement.
* A recent change of senior management.
* A significant change in ownership.
* A significant change in nature or size of the entity's business.
* A change in legal or regulatory requirements.
* A change in the financial reporting framework adopted in the preparation of the
  financial statements.
* A change in other reporting requirements.

Acceptance of a Change in the Terms of the Audit Engagement

Request to Change the Terms of the Audit Engagement (Ref: Para. 14)

A29   A request from the entity for the auditor to change the terms of the audit engagement may result from a change in circumstances affecting the need for the service, a misunderstanding as to the nature of an audit as originally requested or a restriction on the scope of the audit engagement, whether imposed by management or caused by other circumstances. The auditor, as required by paragraph 14, considers the justification given for the request, particularly the implications of a restriction on the scope of the audit engagement.

A30   A change in circumstances that affects the entity's requirements or a misunderstanding concerning the nature of the service originally requested may be considered a reasonable basis for requesting a change in the audit engagement.

A31   In contrast, a change may not be considered reasonable if it appears that the change relates to information that is incorrect, incomplete or otherwise unsatisfactory. An example might be where the auditor is unable to obtain sufficient appropriate audit evidence regarding receivables and the entity asks for the audit engagement to be changed to a review engagement to avoid a qualified opinion or a disclaimer of opinion.

Request to Change to a Review or a Related Service (Ref: Para. 15)

A32   Before agreeing to change an audit engagement to a review or a related service, an auditor who was engaged to perform an audit in accordance with ISAs (UK) may need to assess, in addition to the matters referred to in paragraphs A29–A31 above, any legal or contractual implications of the change.

A33   If the auditor concludes that there is reasonable justification to change the audit engagement to a review or a related service, the audit work performed to the date of change may be relevant to the changed engagement; however, the work required to be performed and the report to be issued would be those appropriate to the revised engagement. In order to avoid confusing the reader, the report on the related service would not include reference to:

(a)   The original audit engagement; or

(b)   Any procedures that may have been performed in the original audit engagement, except where the audit engagement is changed to an engagement to undertake agreed-upon procedures and thus reference to the procedures performed is a normal part of the report.

Statement by Auditor on Ceasing to Hold Office (Ref: Para. 17)

A33-1   The auditor of a limited company in the UK who ceases to hold office as auditor is required to comply with the requirements of Sections 519 and 521 of the Companies Act 2006 regarding the statement to be made by the auditor in relation to ceasing to hold office.

Additional Considerations in Engagement Acceptance

Financial Reporting Standards Supplemented by Law or Regulation (Ref: Para. 18)

In some jurisdictions, law or regulation may supplement the financial reporting standards   **A34**
established by an authorized or recognized standards setting organization with additional
requirements relating to the preparation of financial statements. In those jurisdictions,
the applicable financial reporting framework for the purposes of applying the ISAs
(UK) encompasses both the identified financial reporting framework and such additional
requirements provided they do not conflict with the identified financial reporting
framework. This may, for example, be the case when law or regulation prescribes
disclosures in addition to those required by the financial reporting standards or when they
narrow the range of acceptable choices that can be made within the financial reporting
standards.[20]

Financial Reporting Framework Prescribed by Law or Regulation—Other Matters Affecting Acceptance (Ref: Para. 19)

Law or regulation may prescribe that the wording of the auditor's opinion use the phrases   **A35**
'present fairly, in all material respects' or 'give a true and fair view' in a case where
the auditor concludes that the applicable financial reporting framework prescribed by
law or regulation would otherwise have been unacceptable. In this case, the terms of the
prescribed wording of the auditor's report are significantly different from the requirements
of ISAs (UK) (see paragraph 21).

Auditor's Report Prescribed by Law or Regulation (Ref: Para. 21)

ISAs (UK) require that the auditor shall not represent compliance with ISAs (UK) unless   **A36**
the auditor has complied with all of the ISAs (UK) relevant to the audit.[21] When law
or regulation prescribes the layout or wording of the auditor's report in a form or in
terms that are significantly different from the requirements of ISAs (UK) and the auditor
concludes that additional explanation in the auditor's report cannot mitigate possible
misunderstanding, the auditor may consider including a statement in the auditor's report
that the audit is not conducted in accordance with ISAs (UK). The auditor is, however,
encouraged to apply ISAs (UK), including the ISAs (UK) that address the auditor's report,
to the extent practicable, notwithstanding that the auditor is not permitted to refer to the
audit being conducted in accordance with ISAs (UK).

In the UK, certain small companies are permitted by law to prepare their financial   **A36-1**
statements in accordance with the micro-entities regime[21a] in which those financial
statements are presumed in law to give a true and fair view of the micro-entity's assets,
liabilities, financial position and profit or loss. This financial reporting framework is
not considered to be a fair presentation framework as defined in ISA (UK) 200 (Revised

---

[20] *ISA (UK) 700 (Revised June 2016), paragraph 15, includes a requirement regarding the evaluation of whether the financial statements adequately refer to or describe the applicable financial reporting framework.*

[21] *ISA (UK) 200 (Revised June 2016), paragraph 20.*

[21a] *The micro-entities regime consists of FRS* 105 The Financial Reporting Standard applicable to the Micro-entities Regime and The Small Companies and Groups (Accounts and Directors' Report) Regulations 2008 *(SI 2008/409) amended by* The Small Companies (Micro-Entities' Accounts) Regulations 2013 *(SI 2013/3008) and* The Companies, Partnerships and Groups (Accounts and Reports) Regulations 2015 *(SI 2015/980).*

June 2016)[21b] as it does not explicitly or implicitly acknowledge that to achieve fair presentation of the financial statements it may be necessary for management to either provide additional disclosures beyond those required by the framework or to depart from a requirement of the framework. Accordingly, this financial reporting framework is a compliance framework.

A36-2   Whilst entities eligible to prepare financial statements in accordance with the micro-entities regime are not required by UK legislation to have those financial statements audited, in the rare circumstances that such an audit of financial statements is requested, the auditor is required by law to state whether the financial statements give a true and fair view. In accordance with paragraphs 25 and 26 of ISA (UK) 700 (Revised June 2016) expressing an unmodified opinion in terms of a true and fair view is reserved for financial statements prepared in accordance with a fair presentation framework. Accordingly, there is a risk that the auditor's report may be misunderstood by users as implying that the micro-entities regime is a fair presentation framework. The auditor therefore considers this requirement in light of paragraph 21 of this ISA (UK). It may be possible for the auditor to mitigate the potential misunderstanding through the prominent inclusion of an other matter paragraph addressing this in the auditor's report in accordance with ISA (UK) 706 (Revised June 2016).

Considerations Specific to Public Sector Entities

A37   In the public sector, specific requirements may exist within the legislation governing the audit mandate; for example, the auditor may be required to report directly to a minister, the legislature or the public if the entity attempts to limit the scope of the audit.

Appendix 1   (Ref: Para. A23-24)

Example of an Audit Engagement Letter

The example letter in this Appendix has not been tailored for the UK.

The following is an example of an audit engagement letter for an audit of general purpose financial statements prepared in accordance with International Financial Reporting Standards. This letter is not authoritative but is intended only to be a guide that may be used in conjunction with the considerations outlined in this ISA. It will need to be varied according to individual requirements and circumstances. It is drafted to refer to the audit of financial statements for a single reporting period and would require adaptation if intended or expected to apply to recurring audits (see paragraph 13 of this ISA). It may be appropriate to seek legal advice that any proposed letter is suitable.

***

To the appropriate representative of management or those charged with governance of ABC Company:[22]

[*The objective and scope of the audit*]

[21b] *ISA (UK) 200 (Revised June 2016), paragraph 13(a).*

[22] *The addressees and references in the letter would be those that are appropriate in the circumstances of the engagement, including the relevant jurisdiction. It is important to refer to the appropriate persons – see paragraph A21.*

You[23] have requested that we audit the financial statements of ABC Company, which comprise the statement of financial position as at December 31, 20X1, and the statement of comprehensive income, statement of changes in equity and statement of cash flows for the year then ended, and notes to the financial statements, including a summary of significant accounting policies. We are pleased to confirm our acceptance and our understanding of this audit engagement by means of this letter.

The objectives of our audit are to obtain reasonable assurance about whether the financial statements as a whole are free from material misstatement, whether due to fraud or error, and to issue an auditor's report that includes our opinion. Reasonable assurance is a high level of assurance, but is not a guarantee that an audit conducted in accordance with International Standards on Auditing (ISAs) will always detect a material misstatement when it exists. Misstatements can arise from fraud or error and are considered material if, individually or in the aggregate, they could reasonably be expected to influence the economic decisions of users taken on the basis of these financial statements.

[*The responsibilities of the auditor*]

We will conduct our audit in accordance with ISAs. Those standards require that we comply with ethical requirements. As part of an audit in accordance with ISAs, we exercise professional judgment and maintain professional skepticism throughout the audit. We also:

- Identify and assess the risks of material misstatement of the financial statements, whether due to fraud or error, design and perform audit procedures responsive to those risks, and obtain audit evidence that is sufficient and appropriate to provide a basis for our opinion. The risk of not detecting a material misstatement resulting from fraud is higher than for one resulting from error, as fraud may involve collusion, forgery, intentional omissions, misrepresentations, or the override of internal control.
- Obtain an understanding of internal control relevant to the audit in order to design audit procedures that are appropriate in the circumstances, but not for the purpose of expressing an opinion on the effectiveness of the entity's internal control.[24] However, we will communicate to you in writing concerning any significant deficiencies in internal control relevant to the audit of the financial statements that we have identified during the audit.
- Evaluate the appropriateness of accounting policies used and the reasonableness of accounting estimates and related disclosures made by management
- Conclude on the appropriateness of management's use of the going concern basis of accounting and, based on the audit evidence obtained, whether a material uncertainty exists related to events or conditions that may cast significant doubt on the Company's ability to continue as a going concern. If we conclude that a material uncertainty exists, we are required to draw attention in our auditor's report to the related disclosures in the financial statements or, if such disclosures are inadequate, to modify our opinion. Our conclusions are based on the audit evidence obtained up to the date of our auditor's report. However, future events or conditions may cause the Company to cease to continue as a going concern.
- Evaluate the overall presentation, structure and content of the financial statements, including the disclosures, and whether the financial statements represent the underlying transactions and events in a manner that achieves fair presentation.

---

[23] *Throughout this letter, references to 'you,' 'we,' 'us,' 'management,' 'those charged with governance' and 'auditor' would be used or amended as appropriate in the circumstances.*

[24] *This sentence would be modified, as appropriate, in circumstances when the auditor also has responsibility to issue an opinion on the effectiveness of internal control in conjunction with the audit of the financial statements.*

Because of the inherent limitations of an audit, together with the inherent limitations of internal control, there is an unavoidable risk that some material misstatements may not be detected, even though the audit is properly planned and performed in accordance with ISAs.

[The responsibilities of management and identification of the applicable financial reporting framework (for purposes of this example it is assumed that the auditor has not determined that the law or regulation prescribes those responsibilities in appropriate terms; the descriptions in paragraph 6(b) of this ISA are therefore used).]

Our audit will be conducted on the basis that [management and, where appropriate, those charged with governance][25] acknowledge and understand that they have responsibility:

(a)   For the preparation and fair presentation of the financial statements in accordance with International Financial Reporting Standards;[26]

(b)   For such internal control as [management] determines is necessary to enable the preparation of financial statements that are free from material misstatement, whether due to fraud or error; and

(c)   To provide us with:[27]

  (i)   Access to all information of which [management] is aware that is relevant to the preparation of the financial statements such as records, documentation and other matters;

  (ii)   Additional information that we may request from [management] for the purpose of the audit; and

  (iii)   Unrestricted access to persons within the entity from whom we determine it necessary to obtain audit evidence.

As part of our audit process, we will request from [management and, where appropriate, those charged with governance], written confirmation concerning representations made to us in connection with the audit.

We look forward to full cooperation from your staff during our audit.

[Other relevant information]

[Insert other information, such as fee arrangements, billings and other specific terms, as appropriate.]

[Reporting]

[Insert appropriate reference to the expected form and content of the auditor's report including, if applicable, the reporting on other information in accordance with ISA (UK) 720 (Revised).]

The form and content of our report may need to be amended in the light of our audit findings.

---

[25] *Use terminology as appropriate in the circumstances.*

[26] *Or, if appropriate, 'For the preparation of financial statements that give a true and fair view in accordance with International Financial Reporting Standards.'*

[27] *See paragraph A23 for examples of other matters relating to management's responsibilities that may be included.*

Please sign and return the attached copy of this letter to indicate your acknowledgement of, and agreement with, the arrangements for our audit of the financial statements including our respective responsibilities.

XYZ & Co.

Acknowledged and agreed on behalf of ABC Company by

(signed)

....

Name and Title

Date

Appendix 2　　　(Ref: Para. A10)

Determining the Acceptability of General Purpose Frameworks

Jurisdictions that Do Not Have Authorized or Recognized Standards Setting Organizations or Financial Reporting Frameworks Prescribed by Law or Regulation

As explained in paragraph A10 of this ISA (UK), when an entity is registered or operating　1
in a jurisdiction that does not have an authorized or recognized standards setting organization, or where use of the financial reporting framework is not prescribed by law or regulation, management identifies an applicable financial reporting framework. Practice in such jurisdictions is often to use the financial reporting standards established by one of the organizations described in paragraph A8 of this ISA (UK).

Alternatively, there may be established accounting conventions in a particular jurisdiction　2
that are generally recognized as the financial reporting framework for general purpose financial statements prepared by certain specified entities operating in that jurisdiction. When such a financial reporting framework is adopted, the auditor is required by paragraph 6(a) of this ISA (UK) to determine whether the accounting conventions collectively can be considered to constitute an acceptable financial reporting framework for general purpose financial statements. When the accounting conventions are widely used in a particular jurisdiction, the accounting profession in that jurisdiction may have considered the acceptability of the financial reporting framework on behalf of the auditors. Alternatively, the auditor may make this determination by considering whether the accounting conventions exhibit attributes normally exhibited by acceptable financial reporting frameworks (see paragraph 3 below), or by comparing the accounting conventions to the requirements of an existing financial reporting framework considered to be acceptable (see paragraph 4 below).

Acceptable financial reporting frameworks normally exhibit the following attributes that　3
result in information provided in financial statements that is useful to the intended users:

(a)　Relevance, in that the information provided in the financial statements is relevant to the nature of the entity and the purpose of the financial statements. For example, in the case of a business enterprise that prepares general purpose financial statements, relevance is assessed in terms of the information necessary to meet the common financial information needs of a wide range of users in making economic decisions. These needs are ordinarily met by presenting the financial position, financial performance and cash flows of the business enterprise.

(b)   Completeness, in that transactions and events, account balances and disclosures that could affect conclusions based on the financial statements are not omitted.

(c)   Reliability, in that the information provided in the financial statements:

    (i)   Where applicable, reflects the economic substance of events and transactions and not merely their legal form; and

    (ii)   Results in reasonably consistent evaluation, measurement, presentation and disclosure, when used in similar circumstances.

(d)   Neutrality, in that it contributes to information in the financial statements that is free from bias.

(e)   Understandability, in that the information in the financial statements is clear and comprehensive and not subject to significantly different interpretation.

4   The auditor may decide to compare the accounting conventions to the requirements of an existing financial reporting framework considered to be acceptable. For example, the auditor may compare the accounting conventions to IFRSs. For an audit of a small entity, the auditor may decide to compare the accounting conventions to a financial reporting framework specifically developed for such entities by an authorized or recognized standards setting organization. When the auditor makes such a comparison and differences are identified, the decision as to whether the accounting conventions adopted in the preparation of the financial statements constitute an acceptable financial reporting framework includes considering the reasons for the differences and whether application of the accounting conventions, or the description of the financial reporting framework in the financial statements, could result in financial statements that are misleading.

5   A conglomeration of accounting conventions devised to suit individual preferences is not an acceptable financial reporting framework for general purpose financial statements. Similarly, a compliance framework will not be an acceptable financial reporting framework, unless it is generally accepted in the particular jurisdictions by preparers and users.

International Standard on Auditing (UK) 220 (Revised June 2016)

Quality control for an audit of financial statements

(Effective for audits of financial statements for periods commencing on or after 17 June 2016)

Contents

International Standard on Auditing (UK) (ISA (UK)) 220 (Revised June 2016), *Quality Control for an Audit of Financial Statements*, should be read in conjunction with ISA (UK) 200 (Revised June 2016), *Overall Objectives of the Independent Auditor and the Conduct of an Audit in Accordance with International Standards on Auditing (UK)*.

Introduction

Scope of this ISA (UK)

1   This International Standard on Auditing (UK) (ISA (UK)) deals with the specific responsibilities of the auditor regarding quality control procedures for an audit of financial statements. It also addresses, where applicable, the responsibilities of the engagement quality control reviewer. This ISA (UK) is to be read in conjunction with relevant ethical requirements.

System of Quality Control and Role of Engagement Teams

2   Quality control systems, policies and procedures are the responsibility of the audit firm. Under ISQC (UK) 1 (Revised June 2016), the firm has an obligation to establish and maintain a system of quality control to provide it with reasonable assurance that:

    (a)   The firm and its personnel comply with professional standards and applicable legal and regulatory requirements; and

    (b)   The reports issued by the firm or engagement partners are appropriate in the circumstances.[1]

This ISA (UK) is premised on the basis that the firm is subject to ISQC (UK) 1 (Revised June 2016) or to national requirements that are at least as demanding. (Ref: Para. A1)

3   Within the context of the firm's system of quality control, engagement teams have a responsibility to implement quality control procedures that are applicable to the audit engagement and provide the firm with relevant information to enable the functioning of that part of the firm's system of quality control relating to independence.

4   Engagement teams are entitled to rely on the firm's system of quality control, unless information provided by the firm or other parties suggests otherwise. (Ref: Para. A2)

Effective Date

5   This ISA (UK) is effective for audits of financial statements for periods commencing on or after 17 June 2016. Earlier adoption is permitted.

Objective

6   The objective of the auditor is to implement quality control procedures at the engagement level that provide the auditor with reasonable assurance that:

    (a)   The audit complies with professional standards and applicable legal and regulatory requirements; and

    (b)   The auditor's report issued is appropriate in the circumstances.

Definitions

7   For purposes of the ISAs (UK), the following terms have the meanings attributed below:

    (a)   Engagement partner[2] – The partner or other person in the firm who is responsible for the audit engagement and its performance, and for the auditor's report that is issued

---

[1] *ISQC (UK) 1 (Revised June 2016)*, Quality Control for Firms that Perform Audits and Reviews of Financial Statements, and Other Assurance and Related Services Engagements, *paragraph 11*.

[2] *'Engagement partner,' 'partner,' and 'firm' should be read as referring to their public sector equivalents where relevant.*

on behalf of the firm, and who, where required, has the appropriate authority from a professional, legal or regulatory body.

(b) Engagement quality control review – A process designed to provide an objective evaluation, on or before the date of the auditor's report, of the significant judgments the engagement team made and the conclusions it reached in formulating the auditor's report. The engagement quality control review process is only for audits of financial statements of listed entities and those other audit engagements, if any, for which the firm has determined an engagement quality control review is required.

(c) Engagement quality control reviewer – A partner, other person in the firm, suitably qualified external person, or a team made up of such individuals, none of whom is part of the engagement team, with sufficient and appropriate experience and authority to objectively evaluate the significant judgments the engagement team made and the conclusions it reached in formulating the auditor's report.

(d) Engagement team – All partners and staff performing the engagement, and any individuals engaged by the firm or a network firm who perform audit procedures on the engagement. This excludes an auditor's external expert engaged by the firm or by a network firm.[3] The term 'engagement team' also excludes individuals within the client's internal audit function who provide direct assistance on an audit engagement when the external auditor complies with the requirements of ISA (UK) 610 (Revised June 2013).[4]

(e) Firm – A sole practitioner, partnership or corporation or other entity of professional accountants.

(f) Inspection – In relation to completed audit engagements, procedures designed to provide evidence of compliance by engagement teams with the firm's quality control policies and procedures.

(f)-1 Key audit partner – Is defined in UK legislation[4a] as:

(i) The statutory auditor designated by an audit firm for a particular audit engagement as being primarily responsible for carrying out the statutory audit on behalf of the audit firm; or

(ii) In the case of a group audit, the statutory auditor designated by an audit firm as being primarily responsible for carrying out the statutory audit at the level of the group and the statutory auditor designated at the level of material subsidiaries; or

(iii) The statutory auditor who signs the audit report.

(g) Listed entity – An entity whose shares, stock or debt are quoted or listed on a recognized stock exchange, or are marketed under the regulations of a recognized stock exchange or other equivalent body.

In the UK, this includes any company in which the public can trade shares, stock or debt on the open market, such as those listed on the London Stock Exchange (including those admitted to trading on the Alternative Investments Market) and ISDX Markets. It does not include entities whose quoted or listed shares, stock or debt are in substance not freely transferable or cannot be traded freely by the public or the entity.

---

[3] *ISA (UK) 620 (Revised June 2016),* Using the Work of an Auditor's Expert, *paragraph 6(a), defines the term 'auditor's expert.'*

[4] *ISA 610 (Revised June 2013),* Using the Work of Internal Auditors, *establishes limits on the use of direct assistance. It also acknowledges that the external auditor may be prohibited by law or regulation from obtaining direct assistance from internal auditors. Therefore, the use of direct assistance is restricted to situations where it is permitted. The use of internal auditors to provide direct assistance is prohibited in an audit conducted in accordance with ISAs (UK) – see ISA (UK) 610 (Revised June 2013), paragraph 5-1.*

[4a] *In the UK, Schedule 10 to the Companies Act 2006.*

(h)   Monitoring – A process comprising an ongoing consideration and evaluation of the firm's system of quality control, including a periodic inspection of a selection of completed engagements, designed to provide the firm with reasonable assurance that its system of quality control is operating effectively.

(i)   Network firm – A firm or entity that belongs to a network.

(j)   Network – A larger structure:

    (i)   That is aimed at cooperation, and

    (ii)   That is clearly aimed at profit or cost-sharing or shares common ownership, control or management, common quality control policies and procedures, common business strategy, the use of a common brand name, or a significant part of professional resources.

(k)   Partner – Any individual with authority to bind the firm with respect to the performance of a professional services engagement.

(l)   Personnel – Partners and staff.

(m)   Professional standards – International Standards on Auditing (UK) (ISAs (UK)) and relevant ethical requirements.

(m)-1 Public interest entity – Is defined in UK legislation[4b] as:

    (i)   An issuer whose transferable securities are admitted to trading on a regulated market;[4c]

    (ii)   A credit institution within the meaning given by Article 4(1)(1) of Regulation (EU) No. 575/2013 of the European Parliament and of the Council, other than one listed in Article 2 of Directive 2013/36/EU of the European Parliament and of the Council on access to the activity of credit institutions and investment firms;

    (iii)   An insurance undertaking within the meaning given by Article 2(1) of Council Directive 1991/674/EEC of the European Parliament and of the Council on the annual accounts and consolidated accounts of insurance undertakings.

(n)   Relevant ethical requirements – Ethical requirements to which the engagement team and engagement quality control reviewer are subject, which ordinarily comprise Parts A and B of the International Ethics Standards Board for Accountants' *Code of Ethics for Professional Accountants* (IESBA Code) related to an audit of financial statements together with national requirements that are more restrictive.

> Auditors in the UK are subject to ethical requirements from two sources: the FRC's Ethical Standard concerning the integrity, objectivity and independence of the auditor, and the ethical pronouncements established by the auditor's relevant professional body.

(o)   Staff – Professionals, other than partners, including any experts the firm employs.

(p)   Suitably qualified external person – An individual outside the firm with the competence and capabilities to act as an engagement partner, for example a partner of another firm, or an employee (with appropriate experience) of either a professional accountancy body whose members may perform audits of historical financial information or of an organization that provides relevant quality control services.

[4b] *In the UK, Section 494A of the Companies Act 2006.*

[4c] *In the UK, 'issuer' and 'regulated market' have the same meaning as in Part 6 of the Financial Services and Markets Act 2000.*

Requirements

Leadership Responsibilities for Quality on Audits

The engagement partner shall take responsibility for the overall quality on each audit   **8**
engagement to which that partner is assigned. (Ref: Para. A3)

Relevant Ethical Requirements

Throughout the audit engagement, the engagement partner shall remain alert, through   **9**
observation and making inquiries as necessary, for evidence of non-compliance with
relevant ethical requirements by members of the engagement team. (Ref: Para. A4–A5)

If matters come to the engagement partner's attention through the firm's system of quality   **10**
control or otherwise that indicate that members of the engagement team have not complied
with relevant ethical requirements, the engagement partner, in consultation with others in
the firm, shall determine the appropriate action. (Ref: Para. A5)

Independence

The engagement partner shall form a conclusion on compliance with independence   **11**
requirements that apply to the audit engagement. In doing so, the engagement partner
shall: (Ref: Para. A5)

(a) Obtain relevant information from the firm and, where applicable, network firms,
     to identify and evaluate circumstances and relationships that create threats to
     independence;
(b) Evaluate information on identified breaches, if any, of the firm's independence
     policies and procedures to determine whether they create a threat to independence for
     the audit engagement; and
(c) Take appropriate action to eliminate such threats or reduce them to an acceptable
     level by applying safeguards, or, if considered appropriate, to withdraw from the audit
     engagement, where withdrawal is possible under applicable law or regulation. The
     engagement partner shall promptly report to the firm any inability to resolve the
     matter for appropriate action. (Ref: Para. A6–A7)

Acceptance and Continuance of Client Relationships and Audit Engagements

The engagement partner shall be satisfied that appropriate procedures regarding the   **12**
acceptance and continuance of client relationships and audit engagements have been
followed, and shall determine that conclusions reached in this regard are appropriate.
(Ref: Para. A8–A9)

If the engagement partner obtains information that would have caused the firm to decline   **13**
the audit engagement had that information been available earlier, the engagement partner
shall communicate that information promptly to the firm, so that the firm and the
engagement partner can take the necessary action. (Ref: Para. A9)

Assignment of Engagement Teams

The engagement partner shall be satisfied that the engagement team, and any auditor's   **14**
experts who are not part of the engagement team, collectively have the appropriate
competence and capabilities to:

(a) Perform the audit engagement in accordance with professional standards and applicable legal and regulatory requirements; and

(b) Enable an auditor's report that is appropriate in the circumstances to be issued. (Ref: Para. A10–A12)

Engagement Performance

Direction, Supervision and Performance

15   The engagement partner shall take responsibility for:

(a) The direction, supervision and performance of the audit engagement in compliance with professional standards and applicable legal and regulatory requirements; and (Ref: Para. A13–A15, A20)

(b) The auditor's report being appropriate in the circumstances.

Reviews

16   The engagement partner shall take responsibility for reviews being performed in accordance with the firm's review policies and procedures. (Ref: Para. A16–A17, A20)

17   On or before the date of the auditor's report, the engagement partner shall, through a review of the audit documentation and discussion with the engagement team, be satisfied that sufficient appropriate audit evidence has been obtained to support the conclusions reached and for the auditor's report to be issued. (Ref: Para. A18–A20)

Consultation

18   The engagement partner shall:

(a) Take responsibility for the engagement team undertaking appropriate consultation on difficult or contentious matters;

(b) Be satisfied that members of the engagement team have undertaken appropriate consultation during the course of the engagement, both within the engagement team and between the engagement team and others at the appropriate level within or outside the firm;

(c) Be satisfied that the nature and scope of, and conclusions resulting from, such consultations are agreed with the party consulted; and

(d) Determine that conclusions resulting from such consultations have been implemented. (Ref: Para. A21–A22)

Engagement Quality Control Review

19   For audits of financial statements of listed entities, and those other audit engagements, if any, for which the firm has determined that an engagement quality control review is required, the engagement partner shall:

(a) Determine that an engagement quality control reviewer has been appointed;

(b) Discuss significant matters arising during the audit engagement, including those identified during the engagement quality control review, with the engagement quality control reviewer; and

(c) Not date the auditor's report until the completion of the engagement quality control review. (Ref: Para. A23–A25)

The engagement quality control reviewer shall perform an objective evaluation of the **20** significant judgments made by the engagement team, and the conclusions reached in formulating the auditor's report. This evaluation shall involve:

(a) Discussion of significant matters with the engagement partner;
(b) Review of the financial statements and the proposed auditor's report;
(c) Review of selected audit documentation relating to the significant judgments the engagement team made and the conclusions it reached; and
(d) Evaluation of the conclusions reached in formulating the auditor's report and consideration of whether the proposed auditor's report is appropriate. (Ref: Para. A26–A27a, A29–A31)

For audits of financial statements of listed entities, the engagement quality control reviewer, **21** on performing an engagement quality control review, shall also consider the following:

(a) The engagement team's evaluation of the firm's independence in relation to the audit engagement;
(b) Whether appropriate consultation has taken place on matters involving differences of opinion or other difficult or contentious matters, and the conclusions arising from those consultations; and
(c) Whether audit documentation selected for review reflects the work performed in relation to the significant judgments and supports the conclusions reached. (Ref: Para. A28–A31)

For audits of financial statements of public interest entities, the engagement quality **21R-1** control reviewer, on performing an engagement quality control review,[4d] shall also consider the following elements:

(a) The independence of the firm from the entity;
(b) The significant risks which are relevant to the audit and which the key audit partner(s) has identified during the performance of the audit and the measures that the key audit partner(s) has taken to adequately manage those risks;
(c) The reasoning of the key audit partner(s), in particular with regard to the level of materiality and the significant risks referred to in paragraph 21R-1(b);
(d) Any request for advice to external experts and the implementation of such advice;
(e) The nature and scope of the corrected and uncorrected misstatements in the financial statements that were identified during the carrying out of the audit;
(f) The subjects discussed with the audit committee and management and/or supervisory bodies of the entity;
(g) The subjects discussed with competent authorities[4e] and, where applicable, with other third parties; and
(h) Whether the documents and information selected from the file by the engagement quality control reviewer support the opinion of the key audit partner(s) as expressed in the draft of the auditor's report and the additional report to the audit committee.[4f]

The engagement quality control reviewer shall discuss the results of the review, **21R-2** including the elements assessed in paragraph 21R-1, with the key audit partner(s).

[4d] *The requirement for an engagement quality control review is established in ISQC (UK) 1 (Revised June 2016), paragraph 38R-1.*

[4e] *In the UK, the competent authority designated by law is the Financial Reporting Council.*

[4f] *The requirements for these reports are set out respectively in ISA (UK) 700 (Revised June 2016), Forming an Opinion and Reporting on Financial Statements and ISA (UK) 260 (Revised June 2016), Communication with Those Charged with Governance.*

Differences of Opinion

22   If differences of opinion arise within the engagement team, with those consulted or, where applicable, between the engagement partner and the engagement quality control reviewer, the engagement team shall follow the firm's policies and procedures for dealing with and resolving differences of opinion.

Monitoring

23   An effective system of quality control includes a monitoring process designed to provide the firm with reasonable assurance that its policies and procedures relating to the system of quality control are relevant, adequate, and operating effectively. The engagement partner shall consider the results of the firm's monitoring process as evidenced in the latest information circulated by the firm and, if applicable, other network firms and whether deficiencies noted in that information may affect the audit engagement. (Ref: Para A32–A34)

Documentation

24   The auditor shall include in the audit documentation:[5]

    (a)   Issues identified with respect to compliance with relevant ethical requirements and how they were resolved.

    (b)   Conclusions on compliance with independence requirements that apply to the audit engagement, and any relevant discussions with the firm that support these conclusions.

    (c)   Conclusions reached regarding the acceptance and continuance of client relationships and audit engagements.

    (d)   The nature and scope of, and conclusions resulting from, consultations undertaken during the course of the audit engagement. (Ref: Para. A35)

24D-1   The auditor shall include in the audit documentation:

    (a)   All significant threats to the firm's independence as well as the safeguards applied to mitigate those threats; and

    (b)   Those matters it is required to assess before accepting or continuing a statutory audit engagement in accordance with ISQC (UK) 1 (Revised June 2016).

25   The engagement quality control reviewer shall document, for the audit engagement reviewed, that:

    (a)   The procedures required by the firm's policies on engagement quality control review have been performed;

    (b)   The engagement quality control review has been completed on or before the date of the auditor's report; and

    (c)   The reviewer is not aware of any unresolved matters that would cause the reviewer to believe that the significant judgments the engagement team made and the conclusions it reached were not appropriate.

25R-1   For audits of financial statements of public interest entities, the engagement quality control reviewer shall also record:

    (a)   The oral and written information provided by the key audit partner(s) to support the significant judgments as well as the main findings of the audit procedures carried

---

[5] *ISA (UK) 230 (Revised June 2016)*, Audit Documentation, *paragraphs 8–11, and paragraph A6.*

out and the conclusions drawn from those findings, whether or not at the request of the engagement quality control reviewer; and

(b) The opinions of the key audit partner(s), as expressed in the draft of the reports required by ISA (UK) 260 (Revised June 2016) and ISA (UK) 700 (Revised June 2016).

For audits of financial statements of public interest entities, the auditor and the en-   **25R-2**
gagement quality control reviewer shall keep a record of the results of the engagement quality control review, together with the considerations underlying those results, in the audit documentation.

***

Application and Other Explanatory Material

System of Quality Control and Role of Engagement Teams (Ref: Para. 2)

ISQC (UK) 1 (Revised June 2016), or national requirements that are at least as demanding,   **A1**
deals with the firm's responsibilities to establish and maintain its system of quality control for audit engagements. The system of quality control includes policies and procedures that address each of the following elements:

- Leadership responsibilities for quality within the firm;
- Relevant ethical requirements;
- Acceptance and continuance of client relationships and specific engagements;
- Human resources;
- Engagement performance; and
- Monitoring.

National requirements that deal with the firm's responsibilities to establish and maintain a system of quality control are at least as demanding as ISQC (UK) 1 (Revised June 2016) when they address all the elements referred to in this paragraph and impose obligations on the firm that achieve the aims of the requirements set out in ISQC (UK) 1 (Revised June 2016).

Reliance on the Firm's System of Quality Control (Ref: Para. 4)

Unless information provided by the firm or other parties suggest otherwise, the engagement   **A2**
team may rely on the firm's system of quality control in relation to, for example:

- Competence of personnel through their recruitment and formal training.
- Independence through the accumulation and communication of relevant independence information.
- Maintenance of client relationships through acceptance and continuance systems.
- Adherence to applicable legal and regulatory requirements through the monitoring process.

Leadership Responsibilities for Quality on Audits (Ref: Para. 8)

The actions of the engagement partner and appropriate messages to the other members   **A3**
of the engagement team, in taking responsibility for the overall quality on each audit engagement, emphasize:

(a) The importance to audit quality of:

(i)   Performing work that complies with professional standards and applicable legal and regulatory requirements;

(ii) Complying with the firm's quality control policies and procedures as applicable;

(iii) Issuing auditor's reports that are appropriate in the circumstances; and

(iv) The engagement team's ability to raise concerns without fear of reprisals; and

(b) The fact that quality is essential in performing audit engagements.

A3-1   ISQC (UK) 1 (Revised June 2016)[5a] sets out requirements to ensure that securing audit quality, independence and competence are the main criteria used by the firm to select the engagement partner or key audit partner(s).

Relevant Ethical Requirements

Compliance with Relevant Ethical Requirements (Ref: Para. 9)

A4   The IESBA Code[5b] establishes the fundamental principles of professional ethics, which include:

(a) Integrity;

(b) Objectivity;

(c) Professional competence and due care;

(d) Confidentiality; and

(e) Professional behavior.

Definition of 'Firm,' 'Network' and 'Network Firm' (Ref: Para. 9–11)

A5   The definitions of 'firm,' 'network' or 'network firm' in relevant ethical requirements may differ from those set out in this ISA (UK). For example, the IESBA Code[5b] defines the 'firm' as:

(a) A sole practitioner, partnership or corporation of professional accountants;

(b) An entity that controls such parties through ownership, management or other means; and

(c) An entity controlled by such parties through ownership, management or other means.

The IESBA Code also provides guidance in relation to the terms 'network' and 'network firm.'

In complying with the requirements in paragraphs 9–11, the definitions used in the relevant ethical requirements apply in so far as is necessary to interpret those ethical requirements.

Threats to Independence (Ref: Para. 11(c))

A6   The engagement partner may identify a threat to independence regarding the audit engagement that safeguards may not be able to eliminate or reduce to an acceptable level. In that case, as required by paragraph 11(c), the engagement partner reports to the relevant person(s) within the firm to determine appropriate action, which may include eliminating the activity or interest that creates the threat, or withdrawing from the audit engagement, where withdrawal is possible under applicable law or regulation.

[5a] *ISQC (UK) 1 (Revised June 2016), paragraph 30D-1.*

[5b] *In the UK, auditors are subject to ethical requirements from two sources: the FRC's Ethical Standard concerning the integrity, objectivity and independence of the auditor, and the ethical pronouncements established by the auditor's relevant professional body.*

Considerations Specific to Public Sector Entities

Statutory measures may provide safeguards for the independence of public sector auditors. **A7** However, public sector auditors or audit firms carrying out public sector audits on behalf of the statutory auditor may, depending on the terms of the mandate in a particular jurisdiction, need to adapt their approach in order to promote compliance with the spirit of paragraph 11. This may include, where the public sector auditor's mandate does not permit withdrawal from the engagement, disclosure through a public report, of circumstances that have arisen that would, if they were in the private sector, lead the auditor to withdraw.

Acceptance and Continuance of Client Relationships and Audit Engagements (Ref: Para. 12)

ISQC (UK) 1 (Revised June 2016) requires the firm to obtain information considered **A8** necessary in the circumstances before accepting an engagement with a new client, when deciding whether to continue an existing engagement, and when considering acceptance of a new engagement with an existing client.[6] Information such as the following assists the engagement partner in determining whether the conclusions reached regarding the acceptance and continuance of client relationships and audit engagements are appropriate:

- The integrity of the principal owners, key management and those charged with governance of the entity;
- Whether the engagement team is competent to perform the audit engagement and has the necessary capabilities, including time and resources;
- Whether the firm and the engagement team can comply with relevant ethical requirements; and
- Significant matters that have arisen during the current or previous audit engagement, and their implications for continuing the relationship.

Considerations Specific to Public Sector Entities (Ref: Para. 12–13)

In the public sector, auditors may be appointed in accordance with statutory procedures. **A9** Accordingly, certain of the requirements and considerations regarding the acceptance and continuance of client relationships and audit engagements as set out in paragraphs 12, 13 and A8 may not be relevant. Nonetheless, information gathered as a result of the process described may be valuable to public sector auditors in performing risk assessments and in carrying out reporting responsibilities.

Assignment of Engagement Teams (Ref: Para. 14)

An engagement team includes a person using expertise in a specialized area of accounting **A10** or auditing, whether engaged or employed by the firm, if any, who performs audit procedures on the engagement. However, a person with such expertise is not a member of the engagement team if that person's involvement with the engagement is only consultation. Consultations are addressed in paragraph 18, and paragraph A21–A22.

When considering the appropriate competence and capabilities expected of the engagement **A11** team as a whole, the engagement partner may take into consideration such matters as the team's:

- Understanding of, and practical experience with, audit engagements of a similar nature and complexity through appropriate training and participation.

---

[6] *ISQC (UK) 1 (Revised June 2016), paragraph 27(a).*

- Understanding of professional standards and applicable legal and regulatory requirements.
- Technical expertise, including expertise with relevant information technology and specialized areas of accounting or auditing.
- Knowledge of relevant industries in which the client operates.
- Ability to apply professional judgment.
- Understanding of the firm's quality control policies and procedures.

Considerations Specific to Public Sector Entities

A12   In the public sector, additional appropriate competence may include skills that are necessary to discharge the terms of the audit mandate in a particular jurisdiction. Such competence may include an understanding of the applicable reporting arrangements, including reporting to the legislature or other governing body or in the public interest. The wider scope of a public sector audit may include, for example, some aspects of performance auditing or a comprehensive assessment of compliance with law, regulation or other authority and preventing and detecting fraud and corruption.

Engagement Performance

Direction, Supervision and Performance (Ref: Para. 15(a))

A13   Direction of the engagement team involves informing the members of the engagement team of matters such as:

- Their responsibilities, including the need to comply with relevant ethical requirements, and to plan and perform an audit with professional skepticism as required by ISA (UK) 200 (Revised June 2016).[7]
- Responsibilities of respective partners where more than one partner is involved in the conduct of an audit engagement.
- The objectives of the work to be performed.
- The nature of the entity's business.
- Risk-related issues.
- Problems that may arise.
- The detailed approach to the performance of the engagement.

Discussion among members of the engagement team allows less experienced team members to raise questions with more experienced team members so that appropriate communication can occur within the engagement team.

A14   Appropriate teamwork and training assist less experienced members of the engagement team to clearly understand the objectives of the assigned work.

A15   Supervision includes matters such as:

- Tracking the progress of the audit engagement.
- Considering the competence and capabilities of individual members of the engagement team, including whether they have sufficient time to carry out their work, whether they understand their instructions, and whether the work is being carried out in accordance with the planned approach to the audit engagement.
- Addressing significant matters arising during the audit engagement, considering their significance and modifying the planned approach appropriately.
- Identifying matters for consultation or consideration by more experienced engagement team members during the audit engagement.

---

[7] *ISA (UK) 200 (Revised June 2016),* Overall Objectives of the Independent Auditor and the Conduct of an Audit in Accordance with International Standards on Auditing (UK), *paragraph 15.*

Reviews

Review Responsibilities (Ref: Para. 16)

Under ISQC (UK) 1 (Revised June 2016), the firm's review responsibility policies and **A16** procedures are determined on the basis that work of less experienced team members is reviewed by more experienced team members.[8]

A review consists of consideration whether, for example: **A17**

• The work has been performed in accordance with professional standards and applicable legal and regulatory requirements;
• Significant matters have been raised for further consideration;
• Appropriate consultations have taken place and the resulting conclusions have been documented and implemented;
• There is a need to revise the nature, timing and extent of work performed;
• The work performed supports the conclusions reached and is appropriately documented;
• The evidence obtained is sufficient and appropriate to support the auditor's report; and
• The objectives of the engagement procedures have been achieved.

The Engagement Partner's Review of Work Performed (Ref: Para. 17)

Timely reviews of the following by the engagement partner at appropriate stages during the **A18** engagement allow significant matters to be resolved on a timely basis to the engagement partner's satisfaction on or before the date of the auditor's report:

• Critical areas of judgment, especially those relating to difficult or contentious matters identified during the course of the engagement;
• Significant risks; and
• Other areas the engagement partner considers important.

The engagement partner need not review all audit documentation, but may do so. However, as required by ISA (UK) 230 (Revised June 2016), the partner documents the extent and timing of the reviews.[9]

An engagement partner taking over an audit during the engagement may apply the review **A19** procedures as described in paragraph A18 to review the work performed to the date of a change in order to assume the responsibilities of an engagement partner.

Considerations Relevant Where a Member of the Engagement Team with Expertise in a Specialized Area of Accounting or Auditing Is Used (Ref: Para. 15–17)

Where a member of the engagement team with expertise in a specialized area of accounting **A20** or auditing is used, direction, supervision and review of that engagement team member's work may include matters such as:

• Agreeing with that member the nature, scope and objectives of that member's work; and the respective roles of, and the nature, timing and extent of communication between that member and other members of the engagement team.

---

[8] *ISQC (UK) 1 (Revised June 2016), paragraph 33.*

[9] *ISA (UK) 230 (Revised June 2016), paragraph 9(c).*

- Evaluating the adequacy of that member's work including the relevance and reasonableness of that member's findings or conclusions and their consistency with other audit evidence.

Consultation (Ref: Para. 18)

A21   Effective consultation on significant technical, ethical, and other matters within the firm or, where applicable, outside the firm can be achieved when those consulted:

- Are given all the relevant facts that will enable them to provide informed advice; and
- Have appropriate knowledge, seniority and experience.

A22   It may be appropriate for the engagement team to consult outside the firm, for example, where the firm lacks appropriate internal resources. They may take advantage of advisory services provided by other firms, professional and regulatory bodies, or commercial organizations that provide relevant quality control services.

Engagement Quality Control Review

Completion of the Engagement Quality Control Review before Dating of the Auditor's Report (Ref: Para. 19(c))

A23   ISA (UK) 700 (Revised June 2016) requires the auditor's report to be dated no earlier than the date on which the auditor has obtained sufficient appropriate evidence on which to base the auditor's opinion on the financial statements.[10] In cases of an audit of financial statements of listed entities or when an engagement meets the criteria for an engagement quality control review, such a review assists the auditor in determining whether sufficient appropriate evidence has been obtained.

A24   Conducting the engagement quality control review in a timely manner at appropriate stages during the engagement allows significant matters to be promptly resolved to the engagement quality control reviewer's satisfaction on or before the date of the auditor's report.

A25   Completion of the engagement quality control review means the completion by the engagement quality control reviewer of the requirements in paragraphs 20–21, and where applicable, compliance with paragraph 22. Documentation of the engagement quality control review may be completed after the date of the auditor's report as part of the assembly of the final audit file. ISA (UK) 230 (Revised June 2016) establishes requirements and provides guidance in this regard.[11]

Nature, Extent and Timing of Engagement Quality Control Review (Ref: Para. 20)

A26   Remaining alert for changes in circumstances allows the engagement partner to identify situations in which an engagement quality control review is necessary, even though at the start of the engagement, such a review was not required.

A27   The extent of the engagement quality control review may depend, among other things, on the complexity of the audit engagement, whether the entity is a listed entity, and the risk that the auditor's report might not be appropriate in the circumstances. The performance of an engagement quality control review does not reduce the responsibilities of the engagement partner for the audit engagement and its performance.

---

[10]   *ISA (UK) 700 (Revised June 2016)*, Forming an Opinion and Reporting on Financial Statements, *paragraph 41.*

[11]   *ISA (UK) 230 (Revised June 2016), paragraphs 14–16.*

When ISA (UK) 701[12] applies, the conclusions reached by the engagement team in   **A27a**
formulating the auditor's report include determining:

- The key audit matters to be included in the auditor's report;
- The key audit matters that will not be communicated in the auditor's report in accordance with paragraph 14 of ISA (UK) 701, if any; and
- If applicable, depending on the facts and circumstances of the entity and the audit, that there are no key audit matters to communicate in the auditor's report.

In addition, the review of the proposed auditor's report in accordance with paragraph 20(b) includes consideration of the proposed wording to be included in the Key Audit Matters section.

Engagement Quality Control Review of Listed Entities (Ref: Para. 21)

Other matters relevant to evaluating the significant judgments made by the engagement   **A28**
team that may be considered in an engagement quality control review of a listed entity
include:

- Significant risks identified during the engagement in accordance with ISA (UK) 315 (Revised June 2016),[13] and the responses to those risks in accordance with ISA (UK) 330 (Revised June 2016),[14] including the engagement team's assessment of, and response to, the risk of fraud in accordance with ISA (UK) 240 (Revised June 2016).[15]
- Judgments made, particularly with respect to materiality and significant risks.
- The significance and disposition of corrected and uncorrected misstatements identified during the audit.
- The matters to be communicated to management and those charged with governance and, where applicable, other parties such as regulatory bodies.

These other matters, depending on the circumstances, may also be applicable for
engagement quality control reviews for audits of financial statements of other entities.

Considerations Specific to Smaller Entities (Ref: Para. 20–21)

In addition to the audits of financial statements of listed entities, an engagement quality   **A29**
control review is required for audit engagements that meet the criteria established by the
firm that subjects engagements to an engagement quality control review. In some cases,
none of the firm's audit engagements may meet the criteria that would subject them to
such a review.

Considerations Specific to Public Sector Entities (Ref: Para. 20–21)

In the public sector, a statutorily appointed auditor (for example, an Auditor General,   **A30**
or other suitably qualified person appointed on behalf of the Auditor General), may act
in a role equivalent to that of engagement partner with overall responsibility for public
sector audits. In such circumstances, where applicable, the selection of the engagement

---

[12] *ISA (UK) 701,* Communicating Key Audit Matters in the Auditor's Report.

[13] *ISA (UK) 315 (Revised June 2016),* Identifying and Assessing the Risks of Material Misstatement through Understanding the Entity and Its Environment.

[14] *ISA (UK) 330 (Revised June 2016),* The Auditor's Responses to Assessed Risks.

[15] *ISA (UK) 240 (Revised June 2016),* The Auditor's Responsibilities Relating to Fraud in an Audit of Financial Statements.

quality control reviewer includes consideration of the need for independence from the audited entity and the ability of the engagement quality control reviewer to provide an objective evaluation.

A31   Listed entities as referred to in paragraphs 21 and A28 are not common in the public sector. However, there may be other public sector entities that are significant due to size, complexity or public interest aspects, and which consequently have a wide range of stakeholders. Examples include state owned corporations and public utilities. Ongoing transformations within the public sector may also give rise to new types of significant entities. There are no fixed objective criteria on which the determination of significance is based. Nonetheless, public sector auditors evaluate which entities may be of sufficient significance to warrant performance of an engagement quality control review.

Monitoring (Ref: Para. 23)

A32   ISQC (UK) 1 (Revised June 2016) requires the firm to establish a monitoring process designed to provide it with reasonable assurance that the policies and procedures relating to the system of quality control are relevant, adequate and operating effectively.[16]

A33   In considering deficiencies that may affect the audit engagement, the engagement partner may have regard to measures the firm took to rectify the situation that the engagement partner considers are sufficient in the context of that audit.

A34   A deficiency in the firm's system of quality control does not necessarily indicate that a particular audit engagement was not performed in accordance with professional standards and applicable legal and regulatory requirements, or that the auditor's report was not appropriate.

Documentation

Documentation of Consultations (Ref: Para. 24(d))

A35   Documentation of consultations with other professionals that involve difficult or contentious matters that is sufficiently complete and detailed contributes to an understanding of:

- The issue on which consultation was sought; and
- The results of the consultation, including any decisions taken, the basis for those decisions and how they were implemented.

---

[16] *ISQC (UK) 1 (Revised June 2016), paragraph 48.*

International Standard on Auditing (UK) 230 (Revised June 2016)

Audit documentation

(Effective for audits of financial statements for periods commencing on or after 17 June 2016)

Contents

International Standard on Auditing (UK) (ISA (UK)) 230 (Revised June 2016), *Audit Documentation*, should be read in conjunction with ISA (UK) 200 (Revised June 2016), *Overall Objectives of the Independent Auditor and the Conduct of an Audit in Accordance with International Standards on Auditing (UK)*.

Introduction

Scope of this ISA (UK)

1   This International Standard on Auditing (UK) (ISA (UK)) deals with the auditor's responsibility to prepare audit documentation for an audit of financial statements. The Appendix lists other ISAs (UK) that contain specific documentation requirements and guidance. The specific documentation requirements of other ISAs (UK) do not limit the application of this ISA (UK). Law or regulation may establish additional documentation requirements.

Nature and Purposes of Audit Documentation

2   Audit documentation that meets the requirements of this ISA (UK) and the specific documentation requirements of other relevant ISAs (UK) provides:

(a) Evidence of the auditor's basis for a conclusion about the achievement of the overall objectives of the auditor;[1] and

(b) Evidence that the audit was planned and performed in accordance with ISAs (UK) and applicable legal and regulatory requirements.

3   Audit documentation serves a number of additional purposes, including the following:

- Assisting the engagement team to plan and perform the audit.
- Assisting members of the engagement team responsible for supervision to direct and supervise the audit work, and to discharge their review responsibilities in accordance with ISA (UK) 220 (Revised June 2016).[2]
- Enabling the engagement team to be accountable for its work.
- Retaining a record of matters of continuing significance to future audits.
- Enabling the conduct of quality control reviews and inspections in accordance with ISQC (UK) 1 (Revised June 2016)[3] or national requirements that are at least as demanding.[4]
- Enabling the conduct of external inspections in accordance with applicable legal, regulatory or other requirements.

Effective Date

4   This ISA (UK) is effective for audits of financial statements for periods commencing on or after 17 June 2016. Earlier adoption is permitted.

---

[1] *ISA (UK) 200 (Revised June 2016)*, Overall Objectives of the Independent Auditor and the Conduct of an Audit in Accordance with International Standards on Auditing (UK), *paragraph 11.*

[2] *ISA (UK) 220 (Revised June 2016)*, Quality Control for an Audit of Financial Statements, *paragraphs 15–17.*

[3] *ISQC (UK) 1 (Revised June 2016)*, Quality Control for Firms that Perform Audits and Reviews of Financial Statements, and Other Assurance and Related Services Engagements, *paragraphs 32– 33, 35–38, and 48.*

[4] *ISA (UK) 220 (Revised June 2016), paragraph 2.*

Objective

The objective of the auditor is to prepare documentation that provides: **5**

(a) A sufficient and appropriate record of the basis for the auditor's report; and
(b) Evidence that the audit was planned and performed in accordance with ISAs (UK) and applicable legal and regulatory requirements.

Definitions

For purposes of the ISAs (UK), the following terms have the meanings attributed below: **6**

(a) Audit documentation – The record of audit procedures performed, relevant audit evidence obtained, and conclusions the auditor reached (terms such as 'working papers' or 'workpapers' are also sometimes used).

> In the UK, audit documentation shall include all documents, information, records and other data required by ISQC (UK) 1 (Revised June 2016), ISAs (UK) and applicable legal and regulatory requirements.

(b) Audit file – One or more folders or other storage media, in physical or electronic form, containing the records that comprise the audit documentation for a specific engagement.
(c) Experienced auditor – An individual (whether internal or external to the firm) who has practical audit experience, and a reasonable understanding of:
   (i) Audit processes;
   (ii) ISAs (UK) and applicable legal and regulatory requirements;
   (iii) The business environment in which the entity operates; and
   (iv) Auditing and financial reporting issues relevant to the entity's industry.

Requirements

Timely Preparation of Audit Documentation

The auditor shall prepare audit documentation on a timely basis. (Ref: Para. A1)   **7**

Documentation of the Audit Procedures Performed and Audit Evidence Obtained

Form, Content and Extent of Audit Documentation

The auditor shall prepare audit documentation that is sufficient to enable an experienced   **8**
auditor, having no previous connection with the audit, to understand: (Ref: Para. A2–A5, A16–A17)

(a) The nature, timing and extent of the audit procedures performed to comply with the ISAs (UK) and applicable legal and regulatory requirements; (Ref: Para. A6–A7)
(b) The results of the audit procedures performed, and the audit evidence obtained; and
(c) Significant matters arising during the audit, the conclusions reached thereon, and significant professional judgments made in reaching those conclusions. (Ref: Para. A8–A11)

> The auditor shall retain any other data and documents that are important in supporting   **8D-1**
> the auditor's report as part of the audit documentation.

9   In documenting the nature, timing and extent of audit procedures performed, the auditor shall record:

(a) The identifying characteristics of the specific items or matters tested; (Ref: Para. A12)

(b) Who performed the audit work and the date such work was completed; and

(c) Who reviewed the audit work performed and the date and extent of such review. (Ref: Para. A13)

10   The auditor shall document discussions of significant matters with management, those charged with governance, and others, including the nature of the significant matters discussed and when and with whom the discussions took place. (Ref: Para. A14)

11   If the auditor identified information that is inconsistent with the auditor's final conclusion regarding a significant matter, the auditor shall document how the auditor addressed the inconsistency. (Ref: Para. A15)

Departure from a Relevant Requirement

12   If, in exceptional circumstances, the auditor judges it necessary to depart from a relevant requirement in an ISA (UK), the auditor shall document how the alternative audit procedures performed achieve the aim of that requirement, and the reasons for the departure. (Ref: Para. A18–A19)

Matters Arising after the Date of the Auditor's Report

13   If, in exceptional circumstances, the auditor performs new or additional audit procedures or draws new conclusions after the date of the auditor's report, the auditor shall document: (Ref: Para. A20)

(a) The circumstances encountered;

(b) The new or additional audit procedures performed, audit evidence obtained, and conclusions reached, and their effect on the auditor's report; and

(c) When and by whom the resulting changes to audit documentation were made and reviewed.

Assembly of the Final Audit File

14   The auditor shall assemble the audit documentation in an audit file and complete the administrative process of assembling the final audit file on a timely basis after the date of the auditor's report. (Ref: Para. A21–A22)

> In the UK, the assembly of the final audit file shall be completed no later than 60 days from the date of the auditor's report.

14D-1   The auditor shall retain audit documentation that is important for monitoring compliance with ISAs (UK) and other applicable legal requirements.

15   After the assembly of the final audit file has been completed, the auditor shall not delete or discard audit documentation of any nature before the end of its retention period. (Ref: Para. A23)

16   In circumstances other than those envisaged in paragraph 13 where the auditor finds it necessary to modify existing audit documentation or add new audit documentation after the assembly of the final audit file has been completed, the auditor shall, regardless of the nature of the modifications or additions, document: (Ref: Para. A24)

(a) The specific reasons for making them; and
(b) When and by whom they were made and reviewed.

***

Application and Other Explanatory Material

Timely Preparation of Audit Documentation (Ref: Para. 7)

Preparing sufficient and appropriate audit documentation on a timely basis helps to **A1**
enhance the quality of the audit and facilitates the effective review and evaluation of the
audit evidence obtained and conclusions reached before the auditor's report is finalized.
Documentation prepared after the audit work has been performed is likely to be less
accurate than documentation prepared at the time such work is performed.

Documentation of the Audit Procedures Performed and Audit Evidence Obtained

Form, Content and Extent of Audit Documentation (Ref: Para. 8)

The form, content and extent of audit documentation depend on factors such as: **A2**

* The size and complexity of the entity.
* The nature of the audit procedures to be performed.
* The identified risks of material misstatement.
* The significance of the audit evidence obtained.
* The nature and extent of exceptions identified.
* The need to document a conclusion or the basis for a conclusion not readily
  determinable from the documentation of the work performed or audit evidence
  obtained.
* The audit methodology and tools used.

Audit documentation may be recorded on paper or on electronic or other media. Examples   **A3**
of audit documentation include:

* Audit programs.
* Analyses.
* Issues memoranda.
* Summaries of significant matters.
* Letters of confirmation and representation.
* Checklists.
* Correspondence (including e-mail) concerning significant matters.

The auditor may include abstracts or copies of the entity's records (for example,
significant and specific contracts and agreements) as part of audit documentation. Audit
documentation, however, is not a substitute for the entity's accounting records.

The auditor need not include in audit documentation superseded drafts of working papers   **A4**
and financial statements, notes that reflect incomplete or preliminary thinking, previous
copies of documents corrected for typographical or other errors, and duplicates of
documents.

Oral explanations by the auditor, on their own, do not represent adequate support for the   **A5**
work the auditor performed or conclusions the auditor reached, but may be used to explain
or clarify information contained in the audit documentation.

Documentation of Compliance with ISAs (UK) (Ref: Para. 8(a))

A6   In principle, compliance with the requirements of this ISA (UK) will result in the audit documentation being sufficient and appropriate in the circumstances. Other ISAs (UK) contain specific documentation requirements that are intended to clarify the application of this ISA (UK) in the particular circumstances of those other ISAs (UK). The specific documentation requirements of other ISAs (UK) do not limit the application of this ISA (UK). Furthermore, the absence of a documentation requirement in any particular ISA (UK) is not intended to suggest that there is no documentation that will be prepared as a result of complying with that ISA (UK).

A7   Audit documentation provides evidence that the audit complies with the ISAs (UK). However, it is neither necessary nor practicable for the auditor to document every matter considered, or professional judgment made, in an audit. Further, it is unnecessary for the auditor to document separately (as in a checklist, for example) compliance with matters for which compliance is demonstrated by documents included within the audit file. For example:

- The existence of an adequately documented audit plan demonstrates that the auditor has planned the audit.
- The existence of a signed engagement letter in the audit file demonstrates that the auditor has agreed the terms of the audit engagement with management or, where appropriate, those charged with governance.
- An auditor's report containing an appropriately qualified opinion on the financial statements demonstrates that the auditor has complied with the requirement to express a qualified opinion under the circumstances specified in the ISAs (UK).
- In relation to requirements that apply generally throughout the audit, there may be a number of ways in which compliance with them may be demonstrated within the audit file:

    o   For example, there may be no single way in which the auditor's professional skepticism is documented. But the audit documentation may nevertheless provide evidence of the auditor's exercise of professional skepticism in accordance with the ISAs (UK). Such evidence may include specific procedures performed to corroborate management's responses to the auditor's inquiries.
    o   Similarly, that the engagement partner has taken responsibility for the direction, supervision and performance of the audit in compliance with the ISAs (UK) may be evidenced in a number of ways within the audit documentation. This may include documentation of the engagement partner's timely involvement in aspects of the audit, such as participation in the team discussions required by ISA (UK) 315 (Revised June 2016).[5]

Documentation of Significant Matters and Related Significant Professional Judgments (Ref: Para. 8(c))

A8   Judging the significance of a matter requires an objective analysis of the facts and circumstances. Examples of significant matters include:

- Matters that give rise to significant risks (as defined in ISA (UK) 315 (Revised June 2016)).[6]
- Results of audit procedures indicating (a) that the financial statements could be materially misstated, or (b) a need to revise the auditor's previous assessment of the risks of material misstatement and the auditor's responses to those risks.
- Circumstances that cause the auditor significant difficulty in applying necessary audit procedures.

---

[5] *ISA (UK) 315 (Revised June 2016)*, Identifying and Assessing the Risks of Material Misstatement through Understanding the Entity and Its Environment, *paragraph 10.*

[6] *ISA (UK) 315 (Revised June 2016), paragraph 4(e).*

- Findings that could result in a modification to the audit opinion or the inclusion of an Emphasis of Matter paragraph in the auditor's report.
- Concerns about the entity's ability to continue as a going concern.

An important factor in determining the form, content and extent of audit documentation of significant matters is the extent of professional judgment exercised in performing the work and evaluating the results. Documentation of the professional judgments made, where significant, serves to explain the auditor's conclusions and to reinforce the quality of the judgment. Such matters are of particular interest to those responsible for reviewing audit documentation, including those carrying out subsequent audits when reviewing matters of continuing significance (for example, when performing a retrospective review of accounting estimates).   **A9**

Some examples of circumstances in which, in accordance with paragraph 8, it is appropriate to prepare audit documentation relating to the use of professional judgment include, where the matters and judgments are significant: **A10**

- The rationale for the auditor's conclusion when a requirement provides that the auditor 'shall consider' certain information or factors, and that consideration is significant in the context of the particular engagement.
- The basis for the auditor's conclusion on the reasonableness of areas of subjective judgments (for example, the reasonableness of significant accounting estimates).
- The basis for the auditor's conclusions about the authenticity of a document when further investigation (such as making appropriate use of an expert or of confirmation procedures) is undertaken in response to conditions identified during the audit that caused the auditor to believe that the document may not bc authentic.
- When ISA (UK) 701 applies,77 thc auditor's determination of the key audit matters or the determination that there are no key audit matters to be communicated.

The auditor may consider it helpful to prepare and retain as part of the audit documentation a summary (sometimes known as a completion memorandum) that describes the significant matters identified during the audit and how they were addressed, or that includes cross-references to other relevant supporting audit documentation that provides such information. Such a summary may facilitate effective and efficient reviews and inspections of the audit documentation, particularly for large and complex audits. Further, the preparation of such a summary may assist the auditor's consideration of the significant matters. It may also help thc auditor to consider whether, in light of the audit procedures performed and conclusions reached, there is any individual relevant ISA (UK) objective that the auditor cannot achieve that would prevent the auditor from achieving the overall objectives of the auditor.   **A11**

Identification of Specific Items or Matters Tested, and of the Preparer and Reviewer (Ref: Para. 9)

Recording the identifying characteristics serves a number of purposes. For example, it enables the engagement team to be accountable for its work and facilitates the investigation of exceptions or inconsistencies. Identifying characteristics will vary with the nature of the audit procedure and the item or matter tested. For example: **A12**

- For a detailed test of entity-generated purchase orders, the auditor may identify the documents selected for testing by their dates and unique purchase order numbers.
- For a procedure requiring selection or review of all items over a specific amount from a given population, the auditor may record the scope of the procedure and identify the population (for example, all journal entries over a specified amount from the journal register).

---

[7] *ISA (UK) 701,* Communicating Key Audit Matters in the Independent Auditor's Report.

- For a procedure requiring systematic sampling from a population of documents, the auditor may identify the documents selected by recording their source, the starting point and the sampling interval (for example, a systematic sample of shipping reports selected from the shipping log for the period from April 1 to September 30, starting with report number 12345 and selecting every 125th report).
- For a procedure requiring inquiries of specific entity personnel, the auditor may record the dates of the inquiries and the names and job designations of the entity personnel.
- For an observation procedure, the auditor may record the process or matter being observed, the relevant individuals, their respective responsibilities, and where and when the observation was carried out.

A13   ISA (UK) 220 (Revised June 2016) requires the auditor to review the audit work performed through review of the audit documentation.[8] The requirement to document who reviewed the audit work performed does not imply a need for each specific working paper to include evidence of review. The requirement, however, means documenting what audit work was reviewed, who reviewed such work, and when it was reviewed.

Documentation of Discussions of Significant Matters with Management, Those Charged with Governance, and Others (Ref: Para. 10)

A14   The documentation is not limited to records prepared by the auditor but may include other appropriate records such as minutes of meetings prepared by the entity's personnel and agreed by the auditor. Others with whom the auditor may discuss significant matters may include other personnel within the entity, and external parties, such as persons providing professional advice to the entity.

Documentation of How Inconsistencies have been Addressed (Ref: Para. 11)

A15   The requirement to document how the auditor addressed inconsistencies in information does not imply that the auditor needs to retain documentation that is incorrect or superseded.

Considerations Specific to Smaller Entities (Ref: Para. 8)

A16   The audit documentation for the audit of a smaller entity is generally less extensive than that for the audit of a larger entity. Further, in the case of an audit where the engagement partner performs all the audit work, the documentation will not include matters that might have to be documented solely to inform or instruct members of an engagement team, or to provide evidence of review by other members of the team (for example, there will be no matters to document relating to team discussions or supervision). Nevertheless, the engagement partner complies with the overriding requirement in paragraph 8 to prepare audit documentation that can be understood by an experienced auditor, as the audit documentation may be subject to review by external parties for regulatory or other purposes.

A17   When preparing audit documentation, the auditor of a smaller entity may also find it helpful and efficient to record various aspects of the audit together in a single document, with cross-references to supporting working papers as appropriate. Examples of matters that may be documented together in the audit of a smaller entity include the understanding of the entity and its internal control, the overall audit strategy and audit plan, materiality

---

[8]   *ISA (UK) 220 (Revised June 2016), paragraph 17.*

determined in accordance with ISA (UK) 320 (Revised June 2016),[9] assessed risks, significant matters noted during the audit, and conclusions reached.

Departure from a Relevant Requirement (Ref: Para. 12)

The requirements of the ISAs (UK) are designed to enable the auditor to achieve the objectives specified in the ISAs (UK), and thereby the overall objectives of the auditor. Accordingly, other than in exceptional circumstances, the ISAs (UK) call for compliance with each requirement that is relevant in the circumstances of the audit.

A18

The documentation requirement applies only to requirements that are relevant in the circumstances. A requirement is not relevant[10] only in the cases where:

A19

(a) The entire ISA (UK) is not relevant (for example, if an entity does not have an internal audit function, nothing in ISA (UK) 610 (Revised June 2013)[11] is relevant); or

(b) The requirement is conditional and the condition does not exist (for example, the requirement to modify the auditor's opinion where there is an inability to obtain sufficient appropriate audit evidence, and there is no such inability).

Matters Arising after the Date of the Auditor's Report (Ref: Para. 13)

Examples of exceptional circumstances include facts which become known to the auditor after the date of the auditor's report but which existed at that date and which, if known at that date, might have caused the financial statements to be amended or the auditor to modify the opinion in the auditor's report.[12] The resulting changes to the audit documentation are reviewed in accordance with the review responsibilities set out in ISA (UK) 220 (Revised June 2016),[13] with the engagement partner taking final responsibility for the changes.

A20

Assembly of the Final Audit File (Ref: Para. 14–16)

ISQC (UK) 1 (Revised June 2016) (or national requirements that are at least as demanding) requires firms to establish policies and procedures for the timely completion of the assembly of audit files.[14] An appropriate time limit within which to complete the assembly of the final audit file is ordinarily not more than 60 days after the date of the auditor's report.[15]

A21

The completion of the assembly of the final audit file after the date of the auditor's report is an administrative process that does not involve the performance of new audit procedures or the drawing of new conclusions. Changes may, however, be made to the audit documentation during the final assembly process if they are administrative in nature. Examples of such changes include:

A22

[9] *ISA (UK) 320 (Revised June 2016),* Materiality in Planning and Performing an Audit.

[10] *ISA (UK) 200 (Revised June 2016), paragraph 22.*

[11] *ISA (UK) 610 (Revised June 2013),* Using the Work of Internal Auditors, *paragraph 2.*

[12] *ISA (UK) 560,* Subsequent Events, *paragraph 14.*

[13] *ISA (UK) 220 (Revised June 2016), paragraph 16.*

[14] *ISQC (UK) 1 (Revised June 2016), paragraph 45.*

[15] *ISQC (UK) 1 (Revised June 2016), paragraph A54.*

- Deleting or discarding superseded documentation.
- Sorting, collating and cross-referencing working papers.
- Signing off on completion checklists relating to the file assembly process.
- Documenting audit evidence that the auditor has obtained, discussed and agreed with the relevant members of the engagement team before the date of the auditor's report.

A23   ISQC (UK) 1 (Revised June 2016) (or national requirements that are at least as demanding) requires firms to establish policies and procedures for the retention of engagement documentation.[16] The retention period for audit engagements ordinarily is no shorter than five years from the date of the auditor's report, or, if later, the date of the group auditor's report.[17]

A24   An example of a circumstance in which the auditor may find it necessary to modify existing audit documentation or add new audit documentation after file assembly has been completed is the need to clarify existing audit documentation arising from comments received during monitoring inspections performed by internal or external parties.

---

[16]   *ISQC (UK) 1 (Revised June 2016), paragraph 47.*

[17]   *ISQC (UK) 1 (Revised June 2016), paragraph A61.*
     In the UK, the auditor has regard to specific requirements of the auditor's relevant professional body.

Appendix

(Ref: Para. 1)

Specific Audit Documentation Requirements in Other ISAs (UK)

This appendix identifies paragraphs in other ISAs (UK) that contain specific documentation requirements. The list is not a substitute for considering the requirements and related application and other explanatory material in ISAs (UK).

- ISA (UK) 210 (Revised June 2016), *Agreeing the Terms of Audit Engagements* – paragraphs 10–12
- ISA (UK) 220 (Revised June 2016), *Quality Control for an Audit of Financial Statements* – paragraphs 24–25R-2
- ISA (UK) 240 (Revised June 2016), *The Auditor's Responsibilities Relating to Fraud in an Audit of Financial Statements* – paragraphs 44–47
- ISA (UK) 250 (Revised June 2016), Section A—*Consideration of Laws and Regulations in an Audit of Financial Statements* – paragraph 29
- ISA (UK) 260 (Revised June 2016), Communication with Those Charged with Governance – paragraphs 23 and 23D-1
- ISA (UK) 300 (Revised June 2016), *Planning an Audit of Financial Statements* – paragraph 12
- ISA (UK) 315 (Revised June 2016), *Identifying and Assessing the Risks of Material Misstatement through Understanding the Entity and Its Environment* – paragraph 32
- ISA (UK) 320 (Revised June 2016), *Materiality in Planning and Performing an Audit* – paragraph 14
- ISA (UK) 330 (Revised June 2016), *The Auditor's Responses to Assessed Risks* – paragraphs 28–30
- ISA (UK) 450 (Revised June 2016), *Evaluation of Misstatements Identified During the Audit* – paragraph 15
- ISA (UK) 540 (Revised June 2016), *Auditing Accounting Estimates, Including Fair Value Accounting Estimates, and Related Disclosures* – paragraph 23
- ISA (UK) 550, *Related Parties* – paragraph 28
- ISA (UK) 600 (Revised June 2016), *Special Considerations—Audits of Group Financial Statements (Including the Work of Component Auditors)* – paragraphs 50–50D-3
- ISA (UK) 610 (Revised June 2013), *Using the Work of Internal Auditors* – paragraphs 36 and 37
- ISA (UK) 620 (Revised June 2016), Using the Work of an Auditor's Expert – paragraph 15D-1
- ISA (UK) 701, Communicating Key Audit Matters in the Independent Auditor's Report – paragraph 18
- ISA (UK) 720 (Revised June 2016), *The Auditor's Responsibilities Relating to Other Information* – paragraph 25

International Standard on Auditing (UK) 240 (Revised June 2016)
The auditor's responsibilities relating to fraud in an audit of financial statements

(Effective for audits of financial statements for periods commencing on or after 17 June 2016)

Contents

International Standard on Auditing (UK) (ISA (UK)) 240 (Revised June 2016), *The Auditor's Responsibilities Relating to Fraud in an Audit of Financial Statements* should be read in conjunction with ISA (UK) 200 (Revised June 2016), *Overall Objectives of the Independent Auditor and the Conduct of an Audit in Accordance with International Standards on Auditing (UK)*.

Introduction

Scope of this ISA (UK)

1   This International Standard on Auditing (UK) (ISA (UK)) deals with the auditor's responsibilities relating to fraud in an audit of financial statements. Specifically, it expands on how ISA (UK) 315 (Revised June 2016)[1] and ISA (UK) 330 (Revised June 2016)[2] are to be applied in relation to risks of material misstatement due to fraud.

Characteristics of Fraud

2   Misstatements in the financial statements can arise from either fraud or error. The distinguishing factor between fraud and error is whether the underlying action that results in the misstatement of the financial statements is intentional or unintentional.

3   Although fraud is a broad legal concept, for the purposes of the ISAs (UK), the auditor is concerned with fraud that causes a material misstatement in the financial statements. Two types of intentional misstatements are relevant to the auditor – misstatements resulting from fraudulent financial reporting and misstatements resulting from misappropriation of assets. Although the auditor may suspect or, in rare cases, identify the occurrence of fraud, the auditor does not make legal determinations of whether fraud has actually occurred. (Ref: Para. A1–A6)

Responsibility for the Prevention and Detection of Fraud

4   The primary responsibility for the prevention and detection of fraud rests with both those charged with governance of the entity and management. It is important that management, with the oversight of those charged with governance, place a strong emphasis on fraud prevention, which may reduce opportunities for fraud to take place, and fraud deterrence, which could persuade individuals not to commit fraud because of the likelihood of detection and punishment. This involves a commitment to creating a culture of honesty and ethical behavior which can be reinforced by an active oversight by those charged with governance. Oversight by those charged with governance includes considering the potential for override of controls or other inappropriate influence over the financial reporting process, such as efforts by management to manage earnings in order to influence the perceptions of analysts as to the entity's performance and profitability.

Responsibilities of the Auditor

5   An auditor conducting an audit in accordance with ISAs (UK) is responsible for obtaining reasonable assurance that the financial statements taken as a whole are free from material misstatement, whether caused by fraud or error. Owing to the inherent limitations of an audit, there is an unavoidable risk that some material misstatements of the financial statements may not be detected, even though the audit is properly planned and performed in accordance with the ISAs (UK).[3]

---

[1] *ISA (UK) 315 (Revised June 2016)*, Identifying and Assessing the Risks of Material Misstatement through Understanding the Entity and Its Environment.

[2] *ISA (UK) 330 (Revised June 2016)*, The Auditor's Responses to Assessed Risks.

[3] *ISA (UK) 200 (Revised June 2016)*, Overall Objectives of the Independent Auditor and the Conduct of an Audit in Accordance with International Standards on Auditing (UK), *paragraph A51.*

As described in ISA (UK) 200 (Revised June 2016),[4] the potential effects of inherent   **6**
limitations are particularly significant in the case of misstatement resulting from fraud. The
risk of not detecting a material misstatement resulting from fraud is higher than the risk
of not detecting one resulting from error. This is because fraud may involve sophisticated
and carefully organized schemes designed to conceal it, such as forgery, deliberate failure
to record transactions, or intentional misrepresentations being made to the auditor. Such
attempts at concealment may be even more difficult to detect when accompanied by
collusion. Collusion may cause the auditor to believe that audit evidence is persuasive
when it is, in fact, false. The auditor's ability to detect a fraud depends on factors such
as the skillfulness of the perpetrator, the frequency and extent of manipulation, the
degree of collusion involved, the relative size of individual amounts manipulated, and the
seniority of those individuals involved. While the auditor may be able to identify potential
opportunities for fraud to be perpetrated, it is difficult for the auditor to determine whether
misstatements in judgment areas such as accounting estimates are caused by fraud or error.

Furthermore, the risk of the auditor not detecting a material misstatement resulting from   **7**
management fraud is greater than for employee fraud, because management is frequently
in a position to directly or indirectly manipulate accounting records, present fraudulent
financial information or override control procedures designed to prevent similar frauds by
other employees.

When obtaining reasonable assurance, the auditor is responsible for maintaining   **8**
professional skepticism throughout the audit, considering the potential for management
override of controls and recognizing the fact that audit procedures that are effective for
detecting error may not be effective in detecting fraud. The requirements in this ISA
(UK) are designed to assist the auditor in identifying and assessing the risks of material
misstatement due to fraud and in designing procedures to detect such misstatement.

Effective Date

This ISA (UK) is effective for audits of financial statements for periods commencing on or   **9**
after 17 June 2016. Earlier adoption is permitted.

Objectives

The objectives of the auditor are: **10**

(a)   To identify and assess the risks of material misstatement of the financial statements
      due to fraud;
(b)   To obtain sufficient appropriate audit evidence regarding the assessed risks of
      material misstatement due to fraud, through designing and implementing appropriate
      responses; and
(c)   To respond appropriately to fraud or suspected fraud identified during the audit.

Definitions

For purposes of the ISAs (UK), the following terms have the meanings attributed below: **11**

(a)   Fraud – An intentional act by one or more individuals among management, those
      charged with governance, employees, or third parties, involving the use of deception
      to obtain an unjust or illegal advantage.

---

[4] *ISA (UK) 200 (Revised June 2016), paragraph A51.*

(b) Fraud risk factors – Events or conditions that indicate an incentive or pressure to commit fraud or provide an opportunity to commit fraud.

Requirements

Professional Skepticism

12   In accordance with ISA (UK) 200 (Revised June 2016),[5] the auditor shall maintain professional skepticism throughout the audit, recognizing the possibility that a material misstatement due to fraud could exist, notwithstanding the auditor's past experience of the honesty and integrity of the entity's management and those charged with governance. (Ref: Para. A7–A8)

13   Unless the auditor has reason to believe the contrary, the auditor may accept records and documents as genuine. If conditions identified during the audit cause the auditor to believe that a document may not be authentic or that terms in a document have been modified but not disclosed to the auditor, the auditor shall investigate further. (Ref: Para. A9)

14   Where responses to inquiries of management or those charged with governance are inconsistent, the auditor shall investigate the inconsistencies.

Discussion among the Engagement Team

15   ISA (UK) 315 (Revised June 2016) requires a discussion among the engagement team members and a determination by the engagement partner of which matters are to be communicated to those team members not involved in the discussion.[6] This discussion shall place particular emphasis on how and where the entity's financial statements may be susceptible to material misstatement due to fraud, including how fraud might occur. The discussion shall occur setting aside beliefs that the engagement team members may have that management and those charged with governance are honest and have integrity. (Ref: Para. A10–A11)

Risk Assessment Procedures and Related Activities

16   When performing risk assessment procedures and related activities to obtain an understanding of the entity and its environment, including the entity's internal control, required by ISA (UK) 315 (Revised June 2016),[7] the auditor shall perform the procedures in paragraphs 17–24 to obtain information for use in identifying the risks of material misstatement due to fraud.

Management and Others within the Entity

17   The auditor shall make inquiries of management regarding:

(a) Management's assessment of the risk that the financial statements may be materially misstated due to fraud, including the nature, extent and frequency of such assessments; (Ref: Para. A12–A13)

---

[5] *ISA (UK) 200 (Revised June 2016), paragraph 15.*

[6] *ISA (UK) 315 (Revised June 2016), paragraph 10.*

[7] *ISA (UK) 315 (Revised June 2016), paragraphs 5–24.*

(b) Management's process for identifying and responding to the risks of fraud in the entity, including any specific risks of fraud that management has identified or that have been brought to its attention, or classes of transactions, account balances, or disclosures for which a risk of fraud is likely to exist; (Ref: Para. A14)

(c) Management's communication, if any, to those charged with governance regarding its processes for identifying and responding to the risks of fraud in the entity; and

(d) Management's communication, if any, to employees regarding its views on business practices and ethical behavior.

The auditor shall make inquiries of management, and others within the entity as appropriate, to determine whether they have knowledge of any actual, suspected or alleged fraud affecting the entity. (Ref: Para. A15–A17)   18

For those entities that have an internal audit function, the auditor shall make inquiries of appropriate individuals within the function to determine whether they have knowledge of any actual, suspected or alleged fraud affecting the entity, and to obtain its views about the risks of fraud. (Ref: Para. A18)   19

Those Charged with Governance

Unless all of those charged with governance are involved in managing the entity,[8] the auditor shall obtain an understanding of how those charged with governance exercise oversight of management's processes for identifying and responding to the risks of fraud in the entity and the internal control that management has established to mitigate these risks. (Ref: Para. A19–A21)   20

Unless all of those charged with governance are involved in managing the entity, the auditor shall make inquiries of those charged with governance to determine whether they have knowledge of any actual, suspected or alleged fraud affecting the entity. These inquiries are made in part to corroborate the responses to the inquiries of management.   21

Unusual or Unexpected Relationships Identified

The auditor shall evaluate whether unusual or unexpected relationships that have been identified in performing analytical procedures, including those related to revenue accounts, may indicate risks of material misstatement due to fraud.   22

Other Information

The auditor shall consider whether other information obtained by the auditor indicates risks of material misstatement due to fraud. (Ref: Para. A22)   23

Evaluation of Fraud Risk Factors

The auditor shall evaluate whether the information obtained from the other risk assessment procedures and related activities performed indicates that one or more fraud risk factors are present. While fraud risk factors may not necessarily indicate the existence of fraud, they have often been present in circumstances where frauds have occurred and therefore may indicate risks of material misstatement due to fraud. (Ref: Para. A23–A27)   24

---

[8] *ISA (UK) 260 (Revised June 2016)*, Communication with Those Charged with Governance, *paragraph 13.*

Identification and Assessment of the Risks of Material Misstatement Due to Fraud

25   In accordance with ISA (UK) 315 (Revised June 2016), the auditor shall identify and assess the risks of material misstatement due to fraud at the financial statement level, and at the assertion level for classes of transactions, account balances and disclosures.[9]

26   When identifying and assessing the risks of material misstatement due to fraud, the auditor shall, based on a presumption that there are risks of fraud in revenue recognition, evaluate which types of revenue, revenue transactions or assertions give rise to such risks. Paragraph 47 specifies the documentation required where the auditor concludes that the presumption is not applicable in the circumstances of the engagement and, accordingly, has not identified revenue recognition as a risk of material misstatement due to fraud. (Ref: Para. A28–A30)

27   The auditor shall treat those assessed risks of material misstatement due to fraud as significant risks and accordingly, to the extent not already done so, the auditor shall obtain an understanding of the entity's related controls, including control activities, relevant to such risks. (Ref: Para. A31–A32)

Responses to the Assessed Risks of Material Misstatement Due to Fraud

Overall Responses

28   In accordance with ISA (UK) 330 (Revised June 2016), the auditor shall determine overall responses to address the assessed risks of material misstatement due to fraud at the financial statement level.[10] (Ref: Para. A33)

29   In determining overall responses to address the assessed risks of material misstatement due to fraud at the financial statement level, the auditor shall:

(a)   Assign and supervise personnel taking account of the knowledge, skill and ability of the individuals to be given significant engagement responsibilities and the auditor's assessment of the risks of material misstatement due to fraud for the engagement; (Ref: Para. A34–A35)

(b)   Evaluate whether the selection and application of accounting policies by the entity, particularly those related to subjective measurements and complex transactions, may be indicative of fraudulent financial reporting resulting from management's effort to manage earnings; and

(c)   Incorporate an element of unpredictability in the selection of the nature, timing and extent of audit procedures. (Ref: Para. A36)

Audit Procedures Responsive to Assessed Risks of Material Misstatement Due to Fraud at the Assertion Level

30   In accordance with ISA (UK) 330 (Revised June 2016), the auditor shall design and perform further audit procedures whose nature, timing and extent are responsive to the assessed risks of material misstatement due to fraud at the assertion level.[11] (Ref: Para. A37–A40)

---

[9]   *ISA (UK) 315 (Revised June 2016), paragraph 25.*

[10]   *ISA (UK) 330 (Revised June 2016), paragraph 5.*

[11]   *ISA (UK) 330 (Revised June 2016), paragraph 6.*

Audit Procedures Responsive to Risks Related to Management Override of Controls

Management is in a unique position to perpetrate fraud because of management's ability to 31
manipulate accounting records and prepare fraudulent financial statements by overriding
controls that otherwise appear to be operating effectively. Although the level of risk of
management override of controls will vary from entity to entity, the risk is nevertheless
present in all entities. Due to the unpredictable way in which such override could occur, it
is a risk of material misstatement due to fraud and thus a significant risk.

Irrespective of the auditor's assessment of the risks of management override of controls, 32
the auditor shall design and perform audit procedures to:

(a) Test the appropriateness of journal entries recorded in the general ledger and
    other adjustments made in the preparation of the financial statements. In designing
    and performing audit procedures for such tests, the auditor shall:
    (i)   Make inquiries of individuals involved in the financial reporting process about
           inappropriate or unusual activity relating to the processing of journal entries
           and other adjustments;
    (ii)   Select journal entries and other adjustments made at the end of a reporting
           period; and
    (iii) Consider the need to test journal entries and other adjustments throughout the
           period. (Ref: Para. A41–A44)
(b) Review accounting estimates for biases and evaluate whether the circumstances
    producing the bias, if any, represent a risk of material misstatement due to fraud. In
    performing this review, the auditor shall:
    (i)   Evaluate whether the judgments and decisions made by management in
           making the accounting estimates included in the financial statements, even
           if they are individually reasonable, indicate a possible bias on the part of the
           entity's management that may represent a risk of material misstatement due
           to fraud. If so, the auditor shall reevaluate the accounting estimates taken as a
           whole; and
    (ii)   Perform a retrospective review of management judgments and assumptions
           related to significant accounting estimates reflected in the financial statements
           of the prior year. (Ref: Para. A45–A47)
(c) For significant transactions that are outside the normal course of business for the
    entity, or that otherwise appear to be unusual given the auditor's understanding of the
    entity and its environment and other information obtained during the audit, the auditor
    shall evaluate whether the business rationale (or the lack thereof) of the transactions
    suggests that they may have been entered into to engage in fraudulent financial
    reporting or to conceal misappropriation of assets. (Ref: Para. A48)

The auditor shall determine whether, in order to respond to the identified risks of 33
management override of controls, the auditor needs to perform other audit procedures in
addition to those specifically referred to above (that is, where there are specific additional
risks of management override that are not covered as part of the procedures performed to
address the requirements in paragraph 32).

Evaluation of Audit Evidence (Ref: Para. A49)

The auditor shall evaluate whether analytical procedures that are performed near the end 34
of the audit, when forming an overall conclusion as to whether the financial statements are
consistent with the auditor's understanding of the entity, indicate a previously unrecognized
risk of material misstatement due to fraud. (Ref: Para. A50)

35 If the auditor identifies a misstatement, the auditor shall evaluate whether such a misstatement is indicative of fraud. If there is such an indication, the auditor shall evaluate the implications of the misstatement in relation to other aspects of the audit, particularly the reliability of management representations, recognizing that an instance of fraud is unlikely to be an isolated occurrence. (Ref: Para. A51)

36 If the auditor identifies a misstatement, whether material or not, and the auditor has reason to believe that it is or may be the result of fraud and that management (in particular, senior management) is involved, the auditor shall reevaluate the assessment of the risks of material misstatement due to fraud and its resulting impact on the nature, timing and extent of audit procedures to respond to the assessed risks. The auditor shall also consider whether circumstances or conditions indicate possible collusion involving employees, management or third parties when reconsidering the reliability of evidence previously obtained. (Ref: Para. A52)

37 If the auditor confirms that, or is unable to conclude whether, the financial statements are materially misstated as a result of fraud the auditor shall evaluate the implications for the audit. (Ref: Para. A53)

Auditor Unable to Continue the Engagement

38 If, as a result of a misstatement resulting from fraud or suspected fraud, the auditor encounters exceptional circumstances that bring into question the auditor's ability to continue performing the audit, the auditor shall:

(a) Determine the professional and legal responsibilities applicable in the circumstances, including whether there is a requirement for the auditor to report to the person or persons who made the audit appointment or, in some cases, to regulatory authorities;

(b) Consider whether it is appropriate to withdraw from the engagement, where withdrawal is possible under applicable law or regulation; and

(c) If the auditor withdraws:

(i) Discuss with the appropriate level of management and those charged with governance the auditor's withdrawal from the engagement and the reasons for the withdrawal; and

(ii) Determine whether there is a professional or legal requirement to report to the person or persons who made the audit appointment or, in some cases, to regulatory authorities, the auditor's withdrawal from the engagement and the reasons for the withdrawal. (Ref: Para. A54–A57)

Written Representations

39 The auditor shall obtain written representations from management and, where appropriate, those charged with governance that:

(a) They acknowledge their responsibility for the design, implementation and maintenance of internal control to prevent and detect fraud;

(b) They have disclosed to the auditor the results of management's assessment of the risk that the financial statements may be materially misstated as a result of fraud;

(c) They have disclosed to the auditor their knowledge of fraud or suspected fraud affecting the entity involving:

(i) Management;

(ii) Employees who have significant roles in internal control; or

(iii) Others where the fraud could have a material effect on the financial statements; and

(d) They have disclosed to the auditor their knowledge of any allegations of fraud, or suspected fraud, affecting the entity's financial statements communicated by employees, former employees, analysts, regulators or others. (Ref: Para. A58– A59)

Communications to Management and with Those Charged with Governance

If the auditor has identified a fraud or has obtained information that indicates that a fraud **40** may exist, the auditor shall communicate these matters on a timely basis to the appropriate level of management in order to inform those with primary responsibility for the prevention and detection of fraud of matters relevant to their responsibilities. (Ref: Para. A60)

Unless all of those charged with governance are involved in managing the entity, if the **41** auditor has identified or suspects fraud involving:

(a) management;
(b) employees who have significant roles in internal control; or
(c) others where the fraud results in a material misstatement in the financial statements,

the auditor shall communicate these matters to those charged with governance on a timely basis. If the auditor suspects fraud involving management, the auditor shall communicate these suspicions to those charged with governance and discuss with them the nature, timing and extent of audit procedures necessary to complete the audit. (Ref: Para. A61–A63)

For audits of financial statements of public interest entities, when an auditor suspects **41R-1** or has reasonable grounds to suspect that irregularities, including fraud with regard to the financial statements of the entity, may occur or has occurred, the auditor shall, unless prohibited by law or regulation, inform the entity and invite it to investigate the matter and take appropriate measures to deal with such irregularities and to prevent any recurrence of such irregularities in the future. (Ref: Para. A63-1)

The auditor shall communicate with those charged with governance any other matters **42** related to fraud that are, in the auditor's judgment, relevant to their responsibilities. (Ref: Para. A64)

Communications to Regulatory and Enforcement Authorities

If the auditor has identified or suspects a fraud, the auditor shall determine whether there is **43** a responsibility to report the occurrence or suspicion to a party outside the entity. Although the auditor's professional duty to maintain the confidentiality of client information may preclude such reporting, the auditor's legal responsibilities may override the duty of confidentiality in some circumstances. (Ref: Para. A65–A67)

For audits of financial statements of public interest entities, where the entity does not **43R-1** investigate the matter referred to in paragraph 42R-1S, the auditor shall inform the authorities responsible for investigating such irregularities. (Ref: Para. A66-1–A66-2)

Documentation

The auditor shall include the following in the audit documentation[12] of the auditor's **44** understanding of the entity and its environment and the assessment of the risks of material misstatement required by ISA (UK) 315 (Revised June 2016):[13]

---

[12] *ISA (UK) 230 (Revised June 2016)*, Audit Documentation, *paragraphs 8–11, and paragraph A6.*

[13] *ISA (UK) 315 (Revised June 2016), paragraph 32.*

(a) The significant decisions reached during the discussion among the engagement team regarding the susceptibility of the entity's financial statements to material misstatement due to fraud; and

(b) The identified and assessed risks of material misstatement due to fraud at the financial statement level and at the assertion level.

45   The auditor shall include the following in the audit documentation of the auditor's responses to the assessed risks of material misstatement required by ISA (UK) 330 (Revised June 2016):[14]

(a) The overall responses to the assessed risks of material misstatement due to fraud at the financial statement level and the nature, timing and extent of audit procedures, and the linkage of those procedures with the assessed risks of material misstatement due to fraud at the assertion level; and

(b) The results of the audit procedures, including those designed to address the risk of management override of controls.

46   The auditor shall include in the audit documentation communications about fraud made to management, those charged with governance, regulators and others.

47   If the auditor has concluded that the presumption that there is a risk of material misstatement due to fraud related to revenue recognition is not applicable in the circumstances of the engagement, the auditor shall include in the audit documentation the reasons for that conclusion.

***

Application and Other Explanatory Material

Characteristics of Fraud (Ref: Para. 3)

A1   Fraud, whether fraudulent financial reporting or misappropriation of assets, involves incentive or pressure to commit fraud, a perceived opportunity to do so and some rationalization of the act. For example:

- Incentive or pressure to commit fraudulent financial reporting may exist when management is under pressure, from sources outside or inside the entity, to achieve an expected (and perhaps unrealistic) earnings target or financial outcome – particularly since the consequences to management for failing to meet financial goals can be significant. Similarly, individuals may have an incentive to misappropriate assets, for example, because the individuals are living beyond their means.
- A perceived opportunity to commit fraud may exist when an individual believes internal control can be overridden, for example, because the individual is in a position of trust or has knowledge of specific deficiencies in internal control.
- Individuals may be able to rationalize committing a fraudulent act. Some individuals possess an attitude, character or set of ethical values that allow them knowingly and intentionally to commit a dishonest act. However, even otherwise honest individuals can commit fraud in an environment that imposes sufficient pressure on them.

A2   Fraudulent financial reporting involves intentional misstatements including omissions of amounts or disclosures in financial statements to deceive financial statement users. It can be caused by the efforts of management to manage earnings in order to deceive financial statement users by influencing their perceptions as to the entity's performance and

---

[14] *ISA (UK) 330 (Revised June 2016), paragraph 28.*

profitability. Such earnings management may start out with small actions or inappropriate adjustment of assumptions and changes in judgments by management. Pressures and incentives may lead these actions to increase to the extent that they result in fraudulent financial reporting. Such a situation could occur when, due to pressures to meet market expectations or a desire to maximize compensation based on performance, management intentionally takes positions that lead to fraudulent financial reporting by materially misstating the financial statements. In some entities, management may be motivated to reduce earnings by a material amount to minimize tax or to inflate earnings to secure bank financing.

Fraudulent financial reporting may be accomplished by the following: **A3**

- Manipulation, falsification (including forgery), or alteration of accounting records or supporting documentation from which the financial statements are prepared.
- Misrepresentation in, or intentional omission from, the financial statements of events, transactions or other significant information.
- Intentional misapplication of accounting principles relating to amounts, classification, manner of presentation, or disclosure.

Fraudulent financial reporting often involves management override of controls that   **A4** otherwise may appear to be operating effectively. Fraud can be committed by management overriding controls using such techniques as intentionally:

- Recording fictitious journal entries, particularly close to the end of an accounting period, to manipulate operating results or achieve other objectives.
- Inappropriately adjusting assumptions and changing judgments used to estimate account balances.
- Omitting, advancing or delaying recognition in the financial statements of events and transactions that have occurred during the reporting period.
- Omitting, obscuring or misstating disclosures required by the applicable financial reporting framework, or disclosures that are necessary to achieve fair presentation.
- Concealing facts that could affect the amounts recorded in the financial statements.
- Engaging in complex transactions that are structured to misrepresent the financial position or financial performance of the entity.
- Altering records and terms related to significant and unusual transactions.

Misappropriation of assets involves the theft of an entity's assets and is often perpetrated   **A5** by employees in relatively small and immaterial amounts. However, it can also involve management who are usually more able to disguise or conceal misappropriations in ways that are difficult to detect. Misappropriation of assets can be accomplished in a variety of ways including:

- Embezzling receipts (for example, misappropriating collections on accounts receivable or diverting receipts in respect of written-off accounts to personal bank accounts).
- Stealing physical assets or intellectual property (for example, stealing inventory for personal use or for sale, stealing scrap for resale, colluding with a competitor by disclosing technological data in return for payment).
- Causing an entity to pay for goods and services not received (for example, payments to fictitious vendors, kickbacks paid by vendors to the entity's purchasing agents in return for inflating prices, payments to fictitious employees).
- Using an entity's assets for personal use (for example, using the entity's assets as collateral for a personal loan or a loan to a related party).

Misappropriation of assets is often accompanied by false or misleading records or documents in order to conceal the fact that the assets are missing or have been pledged without proper authorization.

Considerations Specific to Public Sector Entities

A6   The public sector auditor's responsibilities relating to fraud may be a result of law, regulation or other authority applicable to public sector entities or separately covered by the auditor's mandate. Consequently, the public sector auditor's responsibilities may not be limited to consideration of risks of material misstatement of the financial statements, but may also include a broader responsibility to consider risks of fraud.

Professional Skepticism (Ref: Para. 12–14)

A7   Maintaining professional skepticism requires an ongoing questioning of whether the information and audit evidence obtained suggests that a material misstatement due to fraud may exist. It includes considering the reliability of the information to be used as audit evidence and the controls over its preparation and maintenance where relevant. Due to the characteristics of fraud, the auditor's professional skepticism is particularly important when considering the risks of material misstatement due to fraud.

A8   Although the auditor cannot be expected to disregard past experience of the honesty and integrity of the entity's management and those charged with governance, the auditor's professional skepticism is particularly important in considering the risks of material misstatement due to fraud because there may have been changes in circumstances.

A9   An audit performed in accordance with ISAs (UK) rarely involves the authentication of documents, nor is the auditor trained as or expected to be an expert in such authentication.[15] However, when the auditor identifies conditions that cause the auditor to believe that a document may not be authentic or that terms in a document have been modified but not disclosed to the auditor, possible procedures to investigate further may include:

- Confirming directly with the third party.
- Using the work of an expert to assess the document's authenticity.

Discussion among the Engagement Team (Ref: Para. 15)

A10   Discussing the susceptibility of the entity's financial statements to material misstatement due to fraud with the engagement team:

- Provides an opportunity for more experienced engagement team members to share their insights about how and where the financial statements may be susceptible to material misstatement due to fraud.
- Enables the auditor to consider an appropriate response to such susceptibility and to determine which members of the engagement team will conduct certain audit procedures.
- Permits the auditor to determine how the results of audit procedures will be shared among the engagement team and how to deal with any allegations of fraud that may come to the auditor's attention.

A11   The discussion may include such matters as:

- An exchange of ideas among engagement team members about how and where they believe the entity's financial statements (including the individual financial statements and the disclosures) may be susceptible to material misstatement due to fraud, how management could perpetrate and conceal fraudulent financial reporting, and how assets of the entity could be misappropriated.

---

[15] *ISA (UK) 200 (Revised June 2016), paragraph A47.*

- A consideration of circumstances that might be indicative of earnings management and the practices that might be followed by management to manage earnings that could lead to fraudulent financial reporting.
- A consideration of the risk that management may attempt to present disclosures in a manner that may obscure a proper understanding of the matters disclosed (for example, by including too much immaterial information or by using unclear or ambiguous language).
- A consideration of the known external and internal factors affecting the entity that may create an incentive or pressure for management or others to commit fraud, provide the opportunity for fraud to be perpetrated, and indicate a culture or environment that enables management or others to rationalize committing fraud.
- A consideration of management's involvement in overseeing employees with access to cash or other assets susceptible to misappropriation.
- A consideration of any unusual or unexplained changes in behavior or lifestyle of management or employees which have come to the attention of the engagement team.
- An emphasis on the importance of maintaining a proper state of mind throughout the audit regarding the potential for material misstatement due to fraud.
- A consideration of the types of circumstances that, if encountered, might indicate the possibility of fraud.
- A consideration of how an element of unpredictability will be incorporated into the nature, timing and extent of the audit procedures to be performed.
- A consideration of the audit procedures that might be selected to respond to the susceptibility of the entity's financial statement to material misstatement due to fraud and whether certain types of audit procedures are more effective than others.
- A consideration of any allegations of fraud that have come to the auditor's attention.
- A consideration of the risk of management override of controls.

Risk Assessment Procedures and Related Activities

Inquiries of Management

Management's Assessment of the Risk of Material Misstatement Due to Fraud
(Ref: Para. 17(a))

Management[15a] accepts responsibility for the entity's internal control and for the preparation   **A12**
of the entity's financial statements. Accordingly, it is appropriate for the auditor to make inquiries of management regarding management's own assessment of the risk of fraud and the controls in place to prevent and detect it. The nature, extent and frequency of management's assessment of such risk and controls may vary from entity to entity. In some entities, management may make detailed assessments on an annual basis or as part of continuous monitoring. In other entities, management's assessment may be less structured and less frequent. The nature, extent and frequency of management's assessment are relevant to the auditor's understanding of the entity's control environment. For example, the fact that management has not made an assessment of the risk of fraud may in some circumstances be indicative of the lack of importance that management places on internal control.

Considerations specific to smaller entities

In some entities, particularly smaller entities, the focus of management's assessment may   **A13**
be on the risks of employee fraud or misappropriation of assets.

[15a] *In the UK, those charged with governance are responsible for the preparation of the financial statements.*

Management's Process for Identifying and Responding to the Risks of Fraud
(Ref: Para. 17(b))

A14   In the case of entities with multiple locations management's processes may include different levels of monitoring of operating locations, or business segments. Management may also have identified particular operating locations or business segments for which a risk of fraud may be more likely to exist.

Inquiry of Management and Others within the Entity (Ref: Para. 18)

A15   The auditor's inquiries of management may provide useful information concerning the risks of material misstatements in the financial statements resulting from employee fraud. However, such inquiries are unlikely to provide useful information regarding the risks of material misstatement in the financial statements resulting from management fraud. Making inquiries of others within the entity may provide individuals with an opportunity to convey information to the auditor that may not otherwise be communicated.

A16   Examples of others within the entity to whom the auditor may direct inquiries about the existence or suspicion of fraud include:

- Operating personnel not directly involved in the financial reporting process.
- Employees with different levels of authority.
- Employees involved in initiating, processing or recording complex or unusual transactions and those who supervise or monitor such employees.
- In-house legal counsel.
- Chief ethics officer or equivalent person.
- The person or persons charged with dealing with allegations of fraud.

A17   Management is often in the best position to perpetrate fraud. Accordingly, when evaluating management's responses to inquiries with an attitude of professional skepticism, the auditor may judge it necessary to corroborate responses to inquiries with other information.

Inquiries of the Internal Audit Function (Ref: Para. 19)

A18   ISA (UK) 315 (Revised June 2016) and ISA (UK) 610 (Revised June 2013) establish requirements and provide guidance relevant to audits of those entities that have an internal audit function.[16] In carrying out the requirements of those ISAs (UK) in the context of fraud, the auditor may inquire about specific activities of the function including, for example:

- The procedures performed, if any, by the internal audit function during the year to detect fraud.
- Whether management has satisfactorily responded to any findings resulting from those procedures.

Obtaining an Understanding of Oversight Exercised by Those Charged with Governance (Ref: Para. 20)

A19   Those charged with governance of an entity oversee the entity's systems for monitoring risk, financial control and compliance with the law. In many countries, corporate governance practices are well developed and those charged with governance play an active role in oversight of the entity's assessment of the risks of fraud and of the relevant internal

---

[16] *ISA (UK) 315 (Revised June 2016), paragraphs 6(a) and 23, and ISA (UK) 610 (Revised June 2013),* Using the Work of Internal Auditors.

control. Since the responsibilities of those charged with governance and management may vary by entity and by country, it is important that the auditor understands their respective responsibilities to enable the auditor to obtain an understanding of the oversight exercised by the appropriate individuals.[17]

An understanding of the oversight exercised by those charged with governance may provide insights regarding the susceptibility of the entity to management fraud, the adequacy of internal control over risks of fraud, and the competency and integrity of management. The auditor may obtain this understanding in a number of ways, such as by attending meetings where such discussions take place, reading the minutes from such meetings or making inquiries of those charged with governance.   **A20**

Considerations Specific to Smaller Entities

In some cases, all of those charged with governance are involved in managing the entity. This may be the case in a small entity where a single owner manages the entity and no one else has a governance role. In these cases, there is ordinarily no action on the part of the auditor because there is no oversight separate from management.   **A21**

Consideration of Other Information (Ref: Para. 23)

In addition to information obtained from applying analytical procedures, other information obtained about the entity and its environment may be helpful in identifying the risks of material misstatement due to fraud. The discussion among team members may provide information that is helpful in identifying such risks. In addition, information obtained from the auditor's client acceptance and retention processes, and experience gained on other engagements performed for the entity, for example engagements to review interim financial information, may be relevant in the identification of the risks of material misstatement due to fraud.   **A22**

Evaluation of Fraud Risk Factors (Ref: Para. 24)

The fact that fraud is usually concealed can make it very difficult to detect. Nevertheless, the auditor may identify events or conditions that indicate an incentive or pressure to commit fraud or provide an opportunity to commit fraud (fraud risk factors). For example: **A23**

- The need to meet expectations of third parties to obtain additional equity financing may create pressure to commit fraud;
- The granting of significant bonuses if unrealistic profit targets are met may create an incentive to commit fraud; and
- A control environment that is not effective may create an opportunity to commit fraud.

Fraud risk factors cannot easily be ranked in order of importance. The significance of fraud risk factors varies widely. Some of these factors will be present in entities where the specific conditions do not present risks of material misstatement. Accordingly, the determination of whether a fraud risk factor is present and whether it is to be considered in assessing the risks of material misstatement of the financial statements due to fraud requires the exercise of professional judgment.   **A24**

---

[17] *ISA (UK) 260 (Revised June 2016), paragraphs A1–A8, discuss with whom the auditor communicates when the entity's governance structure is not well defined.*

A25   Examples of fraud risk factors related to fraudulent financial reporting and misappropriation of assets are presented in Appendix 1. These illustrative risk factors are classified based on the three conditions that are generally present when fraud exists:

- An incentive or pressure to commit fraud;
- A perceived opportunity to commit fraud; and
- An ability to rationalize the fraudulent action.

Risk factors reflective of an attitude that permits rationalization of the fraudulent action may not be susceptible to observation by the auditor. Nevertheless, the auditor may become aware of the existence of such information. Although the fraud risk factors described in Appendix 1 cover a broad range of situations that may be faced by auditors, they are only examples and other risk factors may exist.

A26   The size, complexity, and ownership characteristics of the entity have a significant influence on the consideration of relevant fraud risk factors. For example, in the case of a large entity, there may be factors that generally constrain improper conduct by management, such as:

- Effective oversight by those charged with governance.
- An effective internal audit function.
- The existence and enforcement of a written code of conduct.

Furthermore, fraud risk factors considered at a business segment operating level may provide different insights when compared with those obtained when considered at an entity-wide level.

Considerations Specific to Smaller Entities

A27   In the case of a small entity, some or all of these considerations may be inapplicable or less relevant. For example, a smaller entity may not have a written code of conduct but, instead, may have developed a culture that emphasizes the importance of integrity and ethical behavior through oral communication and by management example. Domination of management by a single individual in a small entity does not generally, in and of itself, indicate a failure by management to display and communicate an appropriate attitude regarding internal control and the financial reporting process. In some entities, the need for management authorization can compensate for otherwise deficient controls and reduce the risk of employee fraud. However, domination of management by a single individual can be a potential deficiency in internal control since there is an opportunity for management override of controls.

Identification and Assessment of the Risks of Material Misstatement Due to Fraud

Risks of Fraud in Revenue Recognition (Ref: Para. 26)

A28   Material misstatement due to fraudulent financial reporting relating to revenue recognition often results from an overstatement of revenues through, for example, premature revenue recognition or recording fictitious revenues. It may result also from an understatement of revenues through, for example, improperly shifting revenues to a later period.

A29   The risks of fraud in revenue recognition may be greater in some entities than others. For example, there may be pressures or incentives on management to commit fraudulent financial reporting through inappropriate revenue recognition in the case of listed entities when, for example, performance is measured in terms of year-over-year revenue growth or profit. Similarly, for example, there may be greater risks of fraud in revenue recognition in the case of entities that generate a substantial portion of revenues through cash sales.

The presumption that there are risks of fraud in revenue recognition may be rebutted. For example, the auditor may conclude that there is no risk of material misstatement due to fraud relating to revenue recognition in the case where a there is a single type of simple revenue transaction, for example, leasehold revenue from a single unit rental property.   **A30**

Identifying and Assessing the Risks of Material Misstatement Due to Fraud and Understanding the Entity's Related Controls (Ref: Para. 27)

Management may make judgments on the nature and extent of the controls it chooses to implement, and the nature and extent of the risks it chooses to assume.[18] In determining which controls to implement to prevent and detect fraud, management considers the risks that the financial statements may be materially misstated as a result of fraud. As part of this consideration, management may conclude that it is not cost effective to implement and maintain a particular control in relation to the reduction in the risks of material misstatement due to fraud to be achieved.   **A31**

It is therefore important for the auditor to obtain an understanding of the controls that management has designed, implemented and maintained to prevent and detect fraud. In doing so, the auditor may learn, for example, that management has consciously chosen to accept the risks associated with a lack of segregation of duties. Information from obtaining this understanding may also be useful in identifying fraud risks factors that may affect the auditor's assessment of the risks that the financial statements may contain material misstatement due to fraud.   **A32**

Responses to the Assessed Risks of Material Misstatement Due to Fraud

Overall Responses (Ref: Para. 28)

Determining overall responses to address the assessed risks of material misstatement due to fraud generally includes the consideration of how the overall conduct of the audit can reflect increased professional skepticism, for example, through: **A33**

- Increased sensitivity in the selection of the nature and extent of documentation to be examined in support of material transactions.
- Increased recognition of the need to corroborate management explanations or representations concerning material matters.

It also involves more general considerations apart from the specific procedures otherwise planned; these considerations include the matters listed in paragraph 29, which are discussed below.

Assignment and Supervision of Personnel (Ref: Para. 29(a))

The auditor may respond to identified risks of material misstatement due to fraud by, for example, assigning additional individuals with specialized skill and knowledge, such as forensic and IT experts, or by assigning more experienced individuals to the engagement.   **A34**

The extent of supervision reflects the auditor's assessment of risks of material misstatement due to fraud and the competencies of the engagement team members performing the work.   **A35**

---

[18] *ISA (UK) 315 (Revised June 2016), paragraph A55.*

Unpredictability in the Selection of Audit Procedures (Ref: Para. 29(c))

A36   Incorporating an element of unpredictability in the selection of the nature, timing and extent of audit procedures to be performed is important as individuals within the entity who are familiar with the audit procedures normally performed on engagements may be more able to conceal fraudulent financial reporting. This can be achieved by, for example:

●   Performing substantive procedures on selected account balances and assertions not otherwise tested due to their materiality or risk.

●   Adjusting the timing of audit procedures from that otherwise expected.

●   Using different sampling methods.

●   Performing audit procedures at different locations or at locations on an unannounced basis.

Audit Procedures Responsive to Assessed Risks of Material Misstatement Due to Fraud at the Assertion Level (Ref: Para. 30)

A37   The auditor's responses to address the assessed risks of material misstatement due to fraud at the assertion level may include changing the nature, timing and extent of audit procedures in the following ways:

●   The nature of audit procedures to be performed may need to be changed to obtain audit evidence that is more reliable and relevant or to obtain additional corroborative information. This may affect both the type of audit procedures to be performed and their combination. For example:

○   Physical observation or inspection of certain assets may become more important or the auditor may choose to use computer-assisted audit techniques to gather more evidence about data contained in significant accounts or electronic transaction files.

○   The auditor may design procedures to obtain additional corroborative information. For example, if the auditor identifies that management is under pressure to meet earnings expectations, there may be a related risk that management is inflating sales by entering into sales agreements that include terms that preclude revenue recognition or by invoicing sales before delivery. In these circumstances, the auditor may, for example, design external confirmations not only to confirm outstanding amounts, but also to confirm the details of the sales agreements, including date, any rights of return and delivery terms. In addition, the auditor might find it effective to supplement such external confirmations with inquiries of non-financial personnel in the entity regarding any changes in sales agreements and delivery terms.

●   The timing of substantive procedures may need to be modified. The auditor may conclude that performing substantive testing at or near the period end better addresses an assessed risk of material misstatement due to fraud. The auditor may conclude that, given the assessed risks of intentional misstatement or manipulation, audit procedures to extend audit conclusions from an interim date to the period end would not be effective. In contrast, because an intentional misstatement – for example, a misstatement involving improper revenue recognition – may have been initiated in an interim period, the auditor may elect to apply substantive procedures to transactions occurring earlier in or throughout the reporting period.

●   The extent of the procedures applied reflects the assessment of the risks of material misstatement due to fraud. For example, increasing sample sizes or performing analytical procedures at a more detailed level may be appropriate. Also, computer-assisted audit techniques may enable more extensive testing of electronic transactions and account files. Such techniques can be used to select sample transactions from key electronic files, to sort transactions with specific characteristics, or to test an entire population instead of a sample.

If the auditor identifies a risk of material misstatement due to fraud that affects   **A38**
inventory quantities, examining the entity's inventory records may help to identify
locations or items that require specific attention during or after the physical inventory
count. Such a review may lead to a decision to observe inventory counts at certain
locations on an unannounced basis or to conduct inventory counts at all locations on
the same date.

The auditor may identify a risk of material misstatement due to fraud affecting a number of   **A39**
accounts and assertions. These may include asset valuation, estimates relating to specific
transactions (such as acquisitions, restructurings, or disposals of a segment of the business),
and other significant accrued liabilities (such as pension and other post-employment
benefit obligations, or environmental remediation liabilities). The risk may also relate to
significant changes in assumptions relating to recurring estimates. Information gathered
through obtaining an understanding of the entity and its environment may assist the
auditor in evaluating the reasonableness of such management estimates and underlying
judgments and assumptions. A retrospective review of similar management judgments and
assumptions applied in prior periods may also provide insight about the reasonableness of
judgments and assumptions supporting management estimates.

Examples of possible audit procedures to address the assessed risks of material   **A40**
misstatement due to fraud, including those that illustrate the incorporation of an element
of unpredictability, are presented in Appendix 2. The appendix includes examples of
responses to the auditor's assessment of the risks of material misstatement resulting from
both fraudulent financial reporting, including fraudulent financial reporting resulting from
revenue recognition, and misappropriation of assets.

Audit Procedures Responsive to Risks Related to Management Override of Controls

Journal Entries and Other Adjustments (Ref: Para. 32(a))

Material misstatement of financial statements due to fraud often involve the   **A41**
manipulation of the financial reporting process by recording inappropriate or
unauthorized journal entries. This may occur throughout the year or at period end, or
by management making adjustments to amounts reported in the financial statements
that are not reflected in journal entries, such as through consolidating adjustments and
reclassifications.

Further, the auditor's consideration of the risks of material misstatement associated with   **A42**
inappropriate override of controls over journal entries is important since automated
processes and controls may reduce the risk of inadvertent error but do not overcome
the risk that individuals may inappropriately override such automated processes, for
example, by changing the amounts being automatically passed to the general ledger or
to the financial reporting system. Furthermore, where IT is used to transfer information
automatically, there may be little or no visible evidence of such intervention in the
information systems.

When identifying and selecting journal entries and other adjustments for testing and   **A43**
determining the appropriate method of examining the underlying support for the items
selected, the following matters are of relevance:

- *The assessment of the risks of material misstatement due to fraud* – the presence
  of fraud risk factors and other information obtained during the auditor's assessment
  of the risks of material misstatement due to fraud may assist the auditor to identify
  specific classes of journal entries and other adjustments for testing.

- *Controls that have been implemented over journal entries and other adjustments –* effective controls over the preparation and posting of journal entries and other adjustments may reduce the extent of substantive testing necessary, provided that the auditor has tested the operating effectiveness of the controls.
- *The entity's financial reporting process and the nature of evidence that can be obtained –* for many entities routine processing of transactions involves a combination of manual and automated steps and procedures. Similarly, the processing of journal entries and other adjustments may involve both manual and automated procedures and controls. Where information technology is used in the financial reporting process, journal entries and other adjustments may exist only in electronic form.
- *The characteristics of fraudulent journal entries or other adjustments –* inappropriate journal entries or other adjustments often have unique identifying characteristics. Such characteristics may include entries (a) made to unrelated, unusual, or seldom-used accounts, (b) made by individuals who typically do not make journal entries, (c) recorded at the end of the period or as post-closing entries that have little or no explanation or description, (d) made either before or during the preparation of the financial statements that do not have account numbers, or (e) containing round numbers or consistent ending numbers.
- *The nature and complexity of the accounts –* inappropriate journal entries or adjustments may be applied to accounts that (a) contain transactions that are complex or unusual in nature, (b) contain significant estimates and period-end adjustments, (c) have been prone to misstatements in the past, (d) have not been reconciled on a timely basis or contain unreconciled differences, (e) contain intercompany transactions, or (f) are otherwise associated with an identified risk of material misstatement due to fraud. In audits of entities that have several locations or components, consideration is given to the need to select journal entries from multiple locations.
- *Journal entries or other adjustments processed outside the normal course of business –* non standard journal entries may not be subject to the same level of internal control as those journal entries used on a recurring basis to record transactions such as monthly sales, purchases and cash disbursements.

A44   The auditor uses professional judgment in determining the nature, timing and extent of testing of journal entries and other adjustments. However, because fraudulent journal entries and other adjustments are often made at the end of a reporting period, paragraph 32(a)(ii) requires the auditor to select the journal entries and other adjustments made at that time. Further, because material misstatements in financial statements due to fraud can occur throughout the period and may involve extensive efforts to conceal how the fraud is accomplished, paragraph 32(a)(iii) requires the auditor to consider whether there is also a need to test journal entries and other adjustments throughout the period.

Accounting Estimates (Ref: Para. 32(b))

A45   The preparation of the financial statements requires management[14a] to make a number of judgments or assumptions that affect significant accounting estimates and to monitor the reasonableness of such estimates on an ongoing basis. Fraudulent financial reporting is often accomplished through intentional misstatement of accounting estimates. This may be achieved by, for example, understating or overstating all provisions or reserves in the same fashion so as to be designed either to smooth earnings over two or more accounting periods, or to achieve a designated earnings level in order to deceive financial statement users by influencing their perceptions as to the entity's performance and profitability.

A46   The purpose of performing a retrospective review of management judgments and assumptions related to significant accounting estimates reflected in the financial statements of the prior year is to determine whether there is an indication of a possible bias on the part of management. It is not intended to call into question the auditor's professional judgments made in the prior year that were based on information available at the time.

A retrospective review is also required by ISA (UK) 540 (Revised June 2016).[19] That **A47** review is conducted as a risk assessment procedure to obtain information regarding the effectiveness of management's prior period estimation process, audit evidence about the outcome, or where applicable, the subsequent re-estimation of prior period accounting estimates that is pertinent to making current period accounting estimates, and audit evidence of matters, such as estimation uncertainty, that may be required to be disclosed in the financial statements. As a practical matter, the auditor's review of management judgments and assumptions for biases that could represent a risk of material misstatement due to fraud in accordance with this ISA (UK) may be carried out in conjunction with the review required by ISA (UK) 540 (Revised June 2016).

Business Rationale for Significant Transactions (Ref: Para. 32(c))

Indicators that may suggest that significant transactions that are outside the normal course **A48** of business for the entity, or that otherwise appear to be unusual, may have been entered into to engage in fraudulent financial reporting or to conceal misappropriation of assets include:

* The form of such transactions appears overly complex (for example, the transaction involves multiple entities within a consolidated group or multiple unrelated third parties).
* Management has not discussed the nature of and accounting for such transactions with those charged with governance of the entity, and there is inadequate documentation.
* Management is placing more emphasis on the need for a particular accounting treatment than on the underlying economics of the transaction.
* Transactions that involve non-consolidated related parties, including special purpose entities, have not been properly reviewed or approved by those charged with governance of the entity.
* The transactions involve previously unidentified related parties or parties that do not have the substance or the financial strength to support the transaction without assistance from the entity under audit.

Evaluation of Audit Evidence (Ref: Para. 34–37)

ISA (UK) 330 (Revised June 2016) requires the auditor, based on the audit procedures **A49** performed and the audit evidence obtained, to evaluate whether the assessments of the risks of material misstatement at the assertion level remain appropriate.[20] This evaluation is primarily a qualitative matter based on the auditor's judgment. Such an evaluation may provide further insight about the risks of material misstatement due to fraud and whether there is a need to perform additional or different audit procedures. Appendix 3 contains examples of circumstances that may indicate the possibility of fraud.

Analytical Procedures Performed Near the End of the Audit in Forming an Overall Conclusion (Ref: Para. 34)

Determining which particular trends and relationships may indicate a risk of material **A50** misstatement due to fraud requires professional judgment. Unusual relationships involving

---

[19] *ISA (UK) 540 (Revised June 2016)*, Auditing Accounting Estimates, Including Fair Value Accounting Estimates, and Related Disclosures, *paragraph 9*.

[20] *ISA (UK) 330 (Revised June 2016), paragraph 25.*

year-end revenue and income are particularly relevant. These might include, for example: uncharacteristically large amounts of income being reported in the last few weeks of the reporting period or unusual transactions; or income that is inconsistent with trends in cash flow from operations.

Consideration of Identified Misstatements (Ref: Para. 35–37)

A51   Since fraud involves incentive or pressure to commit fraud, a perceived opportunity to do so or some rationalization of the act, an instance of fraud is unlikely to be an isolated occurrence. Accordingly, misstatements, such as numerous misstatements at a specific location even though the cumulative effect is not material, may be indicative of a risk of material misstatement due to fraud.

A52   The implications of identified fraud depend on the circumstances. For example, an otherwise insignificant fraud may be significant if it involves senior management. In such circumstances, the reliability of evidence previously obtained may be called into question, since there may be doubts about the completeness and truthfulness of representations made and about the genuineness of accounting records and documentation. There may also be a possibility of collusion involving employees, management or third parties.

A53   ISA (UK) 450[21] and ISA (UK) 700 (Revised June 2016)[22] establish requirements and provide guidance on the evaluation and disposition of misstatements and the effect on the auditor's opinion in the auditor's report.

Auditor Unable to Continue the Engagement (Ref: Para. 38)

A54   Examples of exceptional circumstances that may arise and that may bring into question the auditor's ability to continue performing the audit include:

- The entity does not take the appropriate action regarding fraud that the auditor considers necessary in the circumstances, even where the fraud is not material to the financial statements;
- The auditor's consideration of the risks of material misstatement due to fraud and the results of audit tests indicate a significant risk of material and pervasive fraud; or
- The auditor has significant concern about the competence or integrity of management or those charged with governance.

A55   Because of the variety of the circumstances that may arise, it is not possible to describe definitively when withdrawal from an engagement is appropriate. Factors that affect the auditor's conclusion include the implications of the involvement of a member of management or of those charged with governance (which may affect the reliability of management representations) and the effects on the auditor of a continuing association with the entity.

A56   The auditor has professional and legal responsibilities in such circumstances and these responsibilities may vary by country. In some countries, for example, the auditor may be entitled to, or required to, make a statement or report to the person or persons who made the audit appointment or, in some cases, to regulatory authorities. Given the exceptional nature of the circumstances and the need to consider the legal requirements, the auditor may consider it appropriate to seek legal advice when deciding whether to withdraw

---

[21]   *ISA (UK) 450,* Evaluation of Misstatements Identified during the Audit.

[22]   *ISA (UK) 700 (Revised June 2016),* Forming an Opinion and Reporting on Financial Statements.

from an engagement and in determining an appropriate course of action, including the possibility of reporting to shareholders, regulators or others.[23]

Considerations Specific to Public Sector Entities

In many cases in the public sector, the option of withdrawing from the engagement may not be available to the auditor due to the nature of the mandate or public interest considerations. **A57**

Written Representations (Ref: Para. 39)

ISA (UK) 580[24] establishes requirements and provides guidance on obtaining appropriate representations from management and, where appropriate, those charged with governance in the audit. In addition to acknowledging that they have fulfilled their responsibility for the preparation of the financial statements, it is important that, irrespective of the size of the entity, management and, where appropriate, those charged with governance acknowledge their responsibility for internal control designed, implemented and maintained to prevent and detect fraud. **A58**

Because of the nature of fraud and the difficulties encountered by auditors in detecting material misstatements in the financial statements resulting from fraud, it is important that the auditor obtain a written representation from management and, where appropriate, those charged with governance confirming that they have disclosed to the auditor: **A59**

(a) The results of management's assessment of the risk that the financial statements may be materially misstated as a result of fraud; and
(b) Their knowledge of actual, suspected or alleged fraud affecting the entity.

Communications to Management and with Those Charged with Governance

Communication to Management (Ref: Para. 40)

When the auditor has obtained evidence that fraud exists or may exist, it is important that the matter be brought to the attention of the appropriate level of management as soon as practicable. This is so even if the matter might be considered inconsequential (for example, a minor defalcation by an employee at a low level in the entity's organization). The determination of which level of management is the appropriate one is a matter of professional judgment and is affected by such factors as the likelihood of collusion and the nature and magnitude of the suspected fraud. Ordinarily, the appropriate level of management is at least one level above the persons who appear to be involved with the suspected fraud. **A60**

Communication with Those Charged with Governance (Ref: Para. 41)

The auditor's communication with those charged with governance may be made orally or in writing. ISA (UK) 260 (Revised June 2016) identifies factors the auditor considers **A61**

---

[23] *The IESBA Code of Ethics for Professional Accountants provides guidance on communications with an auditor replacing the existing auditor.*
In the UK, the relevant ethical guidance on proposed communications with a successor auditor is provided by the ethical pronouncements relating to the work of auditors issued by the auditor's relevant professional body.

[24] *ISA (UK) 580,* Written Representations.

in determining whether to communicate orally or in writing.[25] Due to the nature and sensitivity of fraud involving senior management, or fraud that results in a material misstatement in the financial statements, the auditor reports such matters on a timely basis and may consider it necessary to also report such matters in writing.

A62   In some cases, the auditor may consider it appropriate to communicate with those charged with governance when the auditor becomes aware of fraud involving employees other than management that does not result in a material misstatement. Similarly, those charged with governance may wish to be informed of such circumstances. The communication process is assisted if the auditor and those charged with governance agree at an early stage in the audit about the nature and extent of the auditor's communications in this regard.

A63   In the exceptional circumstances where the auditor has doubts about the integrity or honesty of management or those charged with governance, the auditor may consider it appropriate to obtain legal advice to assist in determining the appropriate course of action.

Communication with Those Charged with Governance of Public Interest Entities (Ref: Para. 41R-1)

A63-1   For audits of financial statements of public interest entities, ISA (UK) 260 (Revised June 2016)[25a] requires the auditor to communicate in the additional report to the audit committee any significant matters involving actual or suspected non-compliance with laws and regulations, including from fraud or suspected fraud, which were identified in the course of the audit.

A63-2   In the UK, laws or regulations may prohibit alerting ('tipping off') the entity when, for example, the auditor is required to report the non-compliance to an appropriate authority pursuant to anti-money laundering legislation.

Other Matters Related to Fraud (Ref: Para. 42)

A64   Other matters related to fraud to be discussed with those charged with governance of the entity may include, for example:

- Concerns about the nature, extent and frequency of management's assessments of the controls in place to prevent and detect fraud and of the risk that the financial statements may be misstated.
- A failure by management to appropriately address identified significant deficiencies in internal control, or to appropriately respond to an identified fraud.
- The auditor's evaluation of the entity's control environment, including questions regarding the competence and integrity of management.
- Actions by management that may be indicative of fraudulent financial reporting, such as management's selection and application of accounting policies that may be indicative of management's effort to manage earnings in order to deceive financial statement users by influencing their perceptions as to the entity's performance and profitability.
- Concerns about the adequacy and completeness of the authorization of transactions that appear to be outside the normal course of business.

---

[25] *ISA (UK) 260 (Revised June 2016), paragraph A38.*

[25a] *ISA (UK) 260 (Revised June 2016), Communication with Those Charged with Governance, paragraph 16R-2(k).*

Communications to Regulatory and Enforcement Authorities
(Ref: Para. 43)

The auditor's professional duty to maintain the confidentiality of client information may preclude reporting fraud to a party outside the client entity. However, the auditor's legal responsibilities vary by country[25b] and, in certain circumstances, the duty of confidentiality may be overridden by statute, the law or courts of law. In some countries, the auditor of a financial institution has a statutory duty to report the occurrence of fraud to supervisory authorities. Also, in some countries the auditor has a duty to report misstatements to authorities in those cases where management and those charged with governance fail to take corrective action.

A65

The auditor may consider it appropriate to obtain legal advice to determine the appropriate course of action in the circumstances, the purpose of which is to ascertain the steps necessary in considering the public interest aspects of identified fraud.

A66

Reporting to Authorities of Public Interest Entities (Ref: Para. 43R-1)

The disclosure in good faith to the authorities responsible for investigating such irregularities, by the auditor, of any irregularities referred to in paragraph 43R-1 shall not constitute a breach of any contractual or legal restriction on disclosure of information in accordance with the Audit Regulation.[25c]

A66-1

The auditor considers whether to take further action when the entity investigates the matter referred to in paragraph 41R-1 but where the measures taken by management or those charged with governance, in the auditor's professional judgement, were not appropriate to deal with the actual or potential risks of fraud identified or would fail to prevent future occurrences of fraud.

A66-2

Considerations Specific to Public Sector Entities

In the public sector, requirements for reporting fraud, whether or not discovered through the audit process, may be subject to specific provisions of the audit mandate or related law, regulation or other authority.

A67

Appendix 1
(Ref: Para. A25)

Examples of Fraud Risk Factors

The fraud risk factors identified in this Appendix are examples of such factors that may be faced by auditors in a broad range of situations. Separately presented are examples relating to the two types of fraud relevant to the auditor's consideration – that is, fraudulent financial reporting and misappropriation of assets. For each of these types of fraud, the risk factors are further classified based on the three conditions generally present when material misstatements due to fraud occur: (a) incentives/pressures, (b) opportunities, and (c) attitudes/rationalizations. Although the risk factors cover a broad range of situations, they are only examples and, accordingly, the auditor may identify additional or different

[25b] *In the UK, anti-money laundering legislation imposes a duty on auditors to report suspected money laundering activity. Suspicions relating to fraud are likely to be required to be reported under this legislation (see paragraph A11-1 in ISA (UK) 250 (Revised June 2016) Section A – Consideration of Laws and Regulations in an Audit of Financial Statements).*

[25c] *Article 7 of Regulation (EU) No 537/2014 of the European Parliament and of the Council of 16 April 2014.*

risk factors. Not all of these examples are relevant in all circumstances, and some may be of greater or lesser significance in entities of different size or with different ownership characteristics or circumstances. Also, the order of the examples of risk factors provided is not intended to reflect their relative importance or frequency of occurrence.

Risk Factors Relating to Misstatements Arising from Fraudulent Financial Reporting

The following are examples of risk factors relating to misstatements arising from fraudulent financial reporting.

Incentives/Pressures

Financial stability or profitability is threatened by economic, industry, or entity operating conditions, such as (or as indicated by):

- High degree of competition or market saturation, accompanied by declining margins.
- High vulnerability to rapid changes, such as changes in technology, product obsolescence, or interest rates.
- Significant declines in customer demand and increasing business failures in either the industry or overall economy.
- Operating losses making the threat of bankruptcy, foreclosure, or hostile takeover imminent.
- Recurring negative cash flows from operations or an inability to generate cash flows from operations while reporting earnings and earnings growth.
- Rapid growth or unusual profitability especially compared to that of other companies in the same industry.
- New accounting, statutory, or regulatory requirements.

Excessive pressure exists for management to meet the requirements or expectations of third parties due to the following:

- Profitability or trend level expectations of investment analysts, institutional investors, significant creditors, or other external parties (particularly expectations that are unduly aggressive or unrealistic), including expectations created by management in, for example, overly optimistic press releases or annual report messages.
- Need to obtain additional debt or equity financing to stay competitive – including financing of major research and development or capital expenditures.
- Marginal ability to meet exchange listing requirements or debt repayment or other debt covenant requirements.
- Perceived or real adverse effects of reporting poor financial results on significant pending transactions, such as business combinations or contract awards.

Information available indicates that the personal financial situation of management or those charged with governance is threatened by the entity's financial performance arising from the following:

- Significant financial interests in the entity.
- Significant portions of their compensation (for example, bonuses, stock options, and earn-out arrangements) being contingent upon achieving aggressive targets for stock price, operating results, financial position, or cash flow.[26]
- Personal guarantees of debts of the entity.

---

[26] *Management incentive plans may be contingent upon achieving targets relating only to certain accounts or selected activities of the entity, even though the related accounts or activities may not be material to the entity as a whole.*

There is excessive pressure on management or operating personnel to meet financial targets established by those charged with governance, including sales or profitability incentive goals.

Opportunities

The nature of the industry or the entity's operations provides opportunities to engage in fraudulent financial reporting that can arise from the following:

- Significant related-party transactions not in the ordinary course of business or with related entities not audited or audited by another firm.
- A strong financial presence or ability to dominate a certain industry sector that allows the entity to dictate terms or conditions to suppliers or customers that may result in inappropriate or non-arm's-length transactions.
- Assets, liabilities, revenues, or expenses based on significant estimates that involve subjective judgments or uncertainties that are difficult to corroborate.
- Significant, unusual, or highly complex transactions, especially those close to period end that pose difficult 'substance over form' questions.
- Significant operations located or conducted across international borders in jurisdictions where differing business environments and cultures exist.
- Use of business intermediaries for which there appears to be no clear business justification.
- Significant bank accounts or subsidiary or branch operations in tax-haven jurisdictions for which there appears to be no clear business justification.

The monitoring of management is not effective as a result of the following:

- Domination of management by a single person or small group (in a non owner-managed business) without compensating controls.
- Oversight by those charged with governance over the financial reporting process and internal control is not effective.

There is a complex or unstable organizational structure, as evidenced by the following:

- Difficulty in determining the organization or individuals that have controlling interest in the entity.
- Overly complex organizational structure involving unusual legal entities or managerial lines of authority.
- High turnover of senior management, legal counsel, or those charged with governance.

Internal control components are deficient as a result of the following:

- Inadequate monitoring of controls, including automated controls and controls over interim financial reporting (where external reporting is required).
- High turnover rates or employment of staff in accounting, information technology, or the internal audit function that are not effective.
- Accounting and information systems that are not effective, including situations involving significant deficiencies in internal control.

Attitudes/Rationalizations

- Communication, implementation, support, or enforcement of the entity's values or ethical standards by management, or the communication of inappropriate values or ethical standards, that are not effective.
- Nonfinancial management's excessive participation in or preoccupation with the selection of accounting policies or the determination of significant estimates.

- Known history of violations of securities laws or other laws and regulations, or claims against the entity, its senior management, or those charged with governance alleging fraud or violations of laws and regulations.
- Excessive interest by management in maintaining or increasing the entity's stock price or earnings trend.
- The practice by management of committing to analysts, creditors, and other third parties to achieve aggressive or unrealistic forecasts.
- Management failing to remedy known significant deficiencies in internal control on a timely basis.
- An interest by management in employing inappropriate means to minimize reported earnings for tax-motivated reasons.
- Low morale among senior management.
- The owner-manager makes no distinction between personal and business transactions.
- Dispute between shareholders in a closely held entity.
- Recurring attempts by management to justify marginal or inappropriate accounting on the basis of materiality.
- The relationship between management and the current or predecessor auditor is strained, as exhibited by the following:
  - Frequent disputes with the current or predecessor auditor on accounting, auditing, or reporting matters.
  - Unreasonable demands on the auditor, such as unrealistic time constraints regarding the completion of the audit or the issuance of the auditor's report.
  - Restrictions on the auditor that inappropriately limit access to people or information or the ability to communicate effectively with those charged with governance.
  - Domineering management behavior in dealing with the auditor, especially involving attempts to influence the scope of the auditor's work or the selection or continuance of personnel assigned to or consulted on the audit engagement.

Risk Factors Arising from Misstatements Arising from Misappropriation of Assets

Risk factors that relate to misstatements arising from misappropriation of assets are also classified according to the three conditions generally present when fraud exists: incentives/pressures, opportunities, and attitudes/rationalization. Some of the risk factors related to misstatements arising from fraudulent financial reporting also may be present when misstatements arising from misappropriation of assets occur. For example, ineffective monitoring of management and other deficiencies in internal control may be present when misstatements due to either fraudulent financial reporting or misappropriation of assets exist. The following are examples of risk factors related to misstatements arising from misappropriation of assets.

Incentives/Pressures

Personal financial obligations may create pressure on management or employees with access to cash or other assets susceptible to theft to misappropriate those assets.

Adverse relationships between the entity and employees with access to cash or other assets susceptible to theft may motivate those employees to misappropriate those assets. For example, adverse relationships may be created by the following:

- Known or anticipated future employee layoffs.
- Recent or anticipated changes to employee compensation or benefit plans.
- Promotions, compensation, or other rewards inconsistent with expectations.

Opportunities

Certain characteristics or circumstances may increase the susceptibility of assets to misappropriation. For example, opportunities to misappropriate assets increase when there are the following:

- Large amounts of cash on hand or processed.
- Inventory items that are small in size, of high value, or in high demand.
- Easily convertible assets, such as bearer bonds, diamonds, or computer chips.
- Fixed assets which are small in size, marketable, or lacking observable identification of ownership.

Inadequate internal control over assets may increase the susceptibility of misappropriation of those assets. For example, misappropriation of assets may occur because there is the following:

- Inadequate segregation of duties or independent checks.
- Inadequate oversight of senior management expenditures, such as travel and other re-imbursements.
- Inadequate management oversight of employees responsible for assets, for example, inadequate supervision or monitoring of remote locations.
- Inadequate job applicant screening of employees with access to assets.
- Inadequate record keeping with respect to assets.
- Inadequate system of authorization and approval of transactions (for example, in purchasing).
- Inadequate physical safeguards over cash, investments, inventory, or fixed assets.
- Lack of complete and timely reconciliations of assets.
- Lack of timely and appropriate documentation of transactions, for example, credits for merchandise returns.
- Lack of mandatory vacations for employees performing key control functions.
- Inadequate management understanding of information technology, which enables information technology employees to perpetrate a misappropriation.
- Inadequate access controls over automated records, including controls over and review of computer systems event logs.

Attitudes/Rationalizations

- Disregard for the need for monitoring or reducing risks related to misappropriations of assets.
- Disregard for internal control over misappropriation of assets by overriding existing controls or by failing to take appropriate remedial action on known deficiencies in internal control.
- Behavior indicating displeasure or dissatisfaction with the entity or its treatment of the employee.
- Changes in behavior or lifestyle that may indicate assets have been misappropriated.
- Tolerance of petty theft.

Appendix 2

(Ref: Para. A40)

Examples of Possible Audit Procedures to Address the Assessed Risks of Material Misstatement Due to Fraud

The following are examples of possible audit procedures to address the assessed risks of material misstatement due to fraud resulting from both fraudulent financial reporting and misappropriation of assets. Although these procedures cover a broad range of situations, they are only examples and, accordingly they may not be the most appropriate nor necessary in each circumstance. Also the order of the procedures provided is not intended to reflect their relative importance.

Consideration at the Assertion Level

Specific responses to the auditor's assessment of the risks of material misstatement due to fraud will vary depending upon the types or combinations of fraud risk factors or conditions identified, and the classes of transactions, account balances, disclosures and assertions they may affect.

The following are specific examples of responses:

- Visiting locations or performing certain tests on a surprise or unannounced basis. For example, observing inventory at locations where auditor attendance has not been previously announced or counting cash at a particular date on a surprise basis.
- Requesting that inventories be counted at the end of the reporting period or on a date closer to period end to minimize the risk of manipulation of balances in the period between the date of completion of the count and the end of the reporting period.
- Altering the audit approach in the current year. For example, contacting major customers and suppliers orally in addition to sending written confirmation, sending confirmation requests to a specific party within an organization, or seeking more or different information.
- Performing a detailed review of the entity's quarter-end or year-end adjusting entries and investigating any that appear unusual as to nature or amount.
- For significant and unusual transactions, particularly those occurring at or near year-end, investigating the possibility of related parties and the sources of financial resources supporting the transactions.
- Performing substantive analytical procedures using disaggregated data. For example, comparing sales and cost of sales by location, line of business or month to expectations developed by the auditor.
- Conducting interviews of personnel involved in areas where a risk of material misstatement due to fraud has been identified, to obtain their insights about the risk and whether, or how, controls address the risk.
- When other independent auditors are auditing the financial statements of one or more subsidiaries, divisions or branches, discussing with them the extent of work necessary to be performed to address the assessed risk of material misstatement due to fraud resulting from transactions and activities among these components.
- If the work of an expert becomes particularly significant with respect to a financial statement item for which the assessed risk of misstatement due to fraud is high, performing additional procedures relating to some or all of the expert's assumptions, methods or findings to determine that the findings are not unreasonable, or engaging another expert for that purpose.
- Performing audit procedures to analyze selected opening balance sheet accounts of previously audited financial statements to assess how certain issues involving

accounting estimates and judgments, for example, an allowance for sales returns, were resolved with the benefit of hindsight.

- Performing procedures on account or other reconciliations prepared by the entity, including considering reconciliations performed at interim periods.
- Performing computer-assisted techniques, such as data mining to test for anomalies in a population.
- Testing the integrity of computer-produced records and transactions.
- Seeking additional audit evidence from sources outside of the entity being audited.

Specific Responses—Misstatement Resulting from Fraudulent Financial Reporting

Examples of responses to the auditor's assessment of the risks of material misstatement due to fraudulent financial reporting are as follows:

Revenue Recognition

- Performing substantive analytical procedures relating to revenue using disaggregated data, for example, comparing revenue reported by month and by product line or business segment during the current reporting period with comparable prior periods. Computer-assisted audit techniques may be useful in identifying unusual or unexpected revenue relationships or transactions.
- Confirming with customers certain relevant contract terms and the absence of side agreements, because the appropriate accounting often is influenced by such terms or agreements and basis for rebates or the period to which they relate are often poorly documented. For example, acceptance criteria, delivery and payment terms, the absence of future or continuing vendor obligations, the right to return the product, guaranteed resale amounts, and cancellation or refund provisions often are relevant in such circumstances.
- Inquiring of the entity's sales and marketing personnel or in-house legal counsel regarding sales or shipments near the end of the period and their knowledge of any unusual terms or conditions associated with these transactions.
- Being physically present at one or more locations at period end to observe goods being shipped or being readied for shipment (or returns awaiting processing) and performing other appropriate sales and inventory cutoff procedures.
- For those situations for which revenue transactions are electronically initiated, processed, and recorded, testing controls to determine whether they provide assurance that recorded revenue transactions occurred and are properly recorded.

Inventory Quantities

- Examining the entity's inventory records to identify locations or items that require specific attention during or after the physical inventory count.
- Observing inventory counts at certain locations on an unannounced basis or conducting inventory counts at all locations on the same date.
- Conducting inventory counts at or near the end of the reporting period to minimize the risk of inappropriate manipulation during the period between the count and the end of the reporting period.

- Performing additional procedures during the observation of the count, for example, more rigorously examining the contents of boxed items, the manner in which the goods are stacked (for example, hollow squares) or labeled, and the quality (that is, purity, grade, or concentration) of liquid substances such as perfumes or specialty chemicals. Using the work of an expert may be helpful in this regard.
- Comparing the quantities for the current period with prior periods by class or category of inventory, location or other criteria, or comparison of quantities counted with perpetual records.
- Using computer-assisted audit techniques to further test the compilation of the physical inventory counts – for example, sorting by tag number to test tag controls or by item serial number to test the possibility of item omission or duplication.

Management Estimates

- Using an expert to develop an independent estimate for comparison to management's estimate.
- Extending inquiries to individuals outside of management and the accounting department to corroborate management's ability and intent to carry out plans that are relevant to developing the estimate.

Specific Responses—Misstatements Due to Misappropriation of Assets

Differing circumstances would necessarily dictate different responses. Ordinarily, the audit response to an assessed risk of material misstatement due to fraud relating to misappropriation of assets will be directed toward certain account balances and classes of transactions. Although some of the audit responses noted in the two categories above may apply in such circumstances, the scope of the work is to be linked to the specific information about the misappropriation risk that has been identified.

Examples of responses to the auditor's assessment of the risk of material misstatements due to misappropriation of assets are as follows:

- Counting cash or securities at or near year-end.
- Confirming directly with customers the account activity (including credit memo and sales return activity as well as dates payments were made) for the period under audit.
- Analyzing recoveries of written-off accounts.
- Analyzing inventory shortages by location or product type.
- Comparing key inventory ratios to industry norm.
- Reviewing supporting documentation for reductions to the perpetual inventory records.
- Performing a computerized match of the vendor list with a list of employees to identify matches of addresses or phone numbers.
- Performing a computerized search of payroll records to identify duplicate addresses, employee identification or taxing authority numbers or bank accounts.
- Reviewing personnel files for those that contain little or no evidence of activity, for example, lack of performance evaluations.
- Analyzing sales discounts and returns for unusual patterns or trends.
- Confirming specific terms of contracts with third parties.
- Obtaining evidence that contracts are being carried out in accordance with their terms.
- Reviewing the propriety of large and unusual expenses.
- Reviewing the authorization and carrying value of senior management and related party loans.
- Reviewing the level and propriety of expense reports submitted by senior management.

Appendix 3

(Ref: Para. A49)

Examples of Circumstances that Indicate the Possibility of Fraud

The following are examples of circumstances that may indicate the possibility that the financial statements may contain a material misstatement resulting from fraud.

Discrepancies in the accounting records, including:

- Transactions that are not recorded in a complete or timely manner or are improperly recorded as to amount, accounting period, classification, or entity policy.
- Unsupported or unauthorized balances or transactions.
- Last-minute adjustments that significantly affect financial results.
- Evidence of employees' access to systems and records inconsistent with that necessary to perform their authorized duties.
- Tips or complaints to the auditor about alleged fraud.

Conflicting or missing evidence, including:

- Missing documents.
- Documents that appear to have been altered.
- Unavailability of other than photocopied or electronically transmitted documents when documents in original form are expected to exist.
- Significant unexplained items on reconciliations.
- Unusual balance sheet changes, or changes in trends or important financial statement ratios or relationships – for example, receivables growing faster than revenues.
- Inconsistent, vague, or implausible responses from management or employees arising from inquiries or analytical procedures.
- Unusual discrepancies between the entity's records and confirmation replies.
- Large numbers of credit entries and other adjustments made to accounts receivable records.
- Unexplained or inadequately explained differences between the accounts receivable sub-ledger and the control account, or between the customer statements and the accounts receivable sub-ledger.
- Missing or non-existent cancelled checks in circumstances where cancelled checks are ordinarily returned to the entity with the bank statement.
- Missing inventory or physical assets of significant magnitude.
- Unavailable or missing electronic evidence, inconsistent with the entity's record retention practices or policies.
- Fewer responses to confirmations than anticipated or a greater number of responses than anticipated.
- Inability to produce evidence of key systems development and program change testing and implementation activities for current-year system changes and deployments.

Problematic or unusual relationships between the auditor and management, including:

- Denial of access to records, facilities, certain employees, customers, vendors, or others from whom audit evidence might be sought.
- Undue time pressures imposed by management to resolve complex or contentious issues.
- Complaints by management about the conduct of the audit or management intimidation of engagement team members, particularly in connection with the auditor's critical assessment of audit evidence or in the resolution of potential disagreements with management.
- Unusual delays by the entity in providing requested information.

- Unwillingness to facilitate auditor access to key electronic files for testing through the use of computer-assisted audit techniques.
- Denial of access to key IT operations staff and facilities, including security, operations, and systems development personnel.
- An unwillingness to add or revise disclosures in the financial statements to make them more complete and understandable.
- An unwillingness to address identified deficiencies in internal control on a timely basis.

Other

- Unwillingness by management to permit the auditor to meet privately with those charged with governance.
- Accounting policies that appear to be at variance with industry norms.
- Frequent changes in accounting estimates that do not appear to result from changed circumstances.
- Tolerance of violations of the entity's code of conduct.

International Standard on Auditing (UK) 250 (Revised June 2016)

Section A – Consideration of laws and regulations in an audit of financial statements

(Effective for audits of financial statements for periods commencing on or after 17 June 2016)

Contents

International Standard on Auditing (UK) (ISA (UK)) 250 (Revised June 2016), *Consideration of Laws and Regulations in an Audit of Financial Statements*, should be read in conjunction with ISA (UK) 200 (Revised June 2016), *Overall Objectives of the Independent Auditor and the Conduct of an Audit in Accordance with International Standards on Auditing (UK)*.

Introduction

Scope of this ISA (UK)

1   This International Standard on Auditing (UK) (ISA (UK)) deals with the auditor's responsibility to consider laws and regulations in an audit of financial statements. This ISA (UK) does not apply to other assurance engagements in which the auditor is specifically engaged to test and report separately on compliance with specific laws or regulations.

1-1   Guidance on the auditor's responsibility to report direct to financial regulators is provided in Section B of this ISA (UK).[1a]

Effect of Laws and Regulations

2   The effect on financial statements of laws and regulations varies considerably. Those laws and regulations to which an entity is subject constitute the legal and regulatory framework. The provisions of some laws or regulations have a direct effect on the financial statements in that they determine the reported amounts and disclosures in an entity's financial statements. Other laws or regulations are to be complied with by management or set the provisions under which the entity is allowed to conduct its business but do not have a direct effect on an entity's financial statements. Some entities operate in heavily regulated industries (such as banks and chemical companies). Others are subject only to the many laws and regulations that relate generally to the operating aspects of the business (such as those related to occupational safety and health, and equal employment opportunity). Non-compliance with laws and regulations may result in fines, litigation or other consequences for the entity that may have a material effect on the financial statements.

Responsibility for Compliance with Laws and Regulations
(Ref: Para. A1–A6)

3   It is the responsibility of management, with the oversight of those charged with governance, to ensure that the entity's operations are conducted in accordance with the provisions of laws and regulations, including compliance with the provisions of laws and regulations that determine the reported amounts and disclosures in an entity's financial statements.[1b]

Responsibility of the Auditor

4   The requirements in this ISA (UK) are designed to assist the auditor in identifying material misstatement of the financial statements due to non-compliance with laws and regulations. However, the auditor is not responsible for preventing non-compliance and cannot be expected to detect non-compliance with all laws and regulations.

5   The auditor is responsible for obtaining reasonable assurance that the financial statements, taken as a whole, are free from material misstatement, whether caused by fraud or error.[1] In conducting an audit of financial statements, the auditor takes into account the applicable legal and regulatory framework. Owing to the inherent limitations of an audit, there is an unavoidable risk that some material misstatements in the financial statements may not be detected, even though the audit is properly planned and performed in accordance with

---

[1a] *ISA (UK) 250 (Revised June 2016), Section B—The Auditor's Statutory Right and Duty to Report to Regulators of Public Interest Entities and Regulators of Other Entities in the Financial Sector.*

[1b] *In the UK, those charged with governance are responsible for the preparation of the financial statements.*

[1] *ISA (UK) 200 (Revised June 2016),* Overall Objectives of the Independent Auditor and the Conduct of an Audit in Accordance with International Standards on Auditing (UK), *paragraph 5.*

the ISAs (UK).[2] In the context of laws and regulations, the potential effects of inherent limitations on the auditor's ability to detect material misstatements are greater for such reasons as the following:

- There are many laws and regulations, relating principally to the operating aspects of an entity, that typically do not affect the financial statements and are not captured by the entity's information systems relevant to financial reporting.
- Non-compliance may involve conduct designed to conceal it, such as collusion, forgery, deliberate failure to record transactions, management override of controls or intentional misrepresentations being made to the auditor.
- Whether an act constitutes non-compliance is ultimately a matter for legal determination by a court of law.

Ordinarily, the further removed non-compliance is from the events and transactions reflected in the financial statements, the less likely the auditor is to become aware of it or to recognize the non-compliance.

This ISA (UK) distinguishes the auditor's responsibilities in relation to compliance with two different categories of laws and regulations as follows: **6**

(a) The provisions of those laws and regulations generally recognized to have a direct effect on the determination of material amounts and disclosures in the financial statements such as tax and pension laws and regulations (see paragraph 13); and
(b) Other laws and regulations that do not have a direct effect on the determination of the amounts and disclosures in the financial statements, but compliance with which may be fundamental to the operating aspects of the business, to an entity's ability to continue its business, or to avoid material penalties (for example, compliance with the terms of an operating license, compliance with regulatory solvency requirements, or compliance with environmental regulations); non-compliance with such laws and regulations may therefore have a material effect on the financial statements (see paragraph 14).

In this ISA (UK), differing requirements are specified for each of the above categories   **7**
of laws and regulations. For the category referred to in paragraph 6(a), the auditor's responsibility is to obtain sufficient appropriate audit evidence regarding compliance with the provisions of those laws and regulations. For the category referred to in paragraph 6(b), the auditor's responsibility is limited to undertaking specified audit procedures to help identify non-compliance with those laws and regulations that may have a material effect on the financial statements.

The auditor is required by this ISA (UK) to remain alert to the possibility that other audit   **8**
procedures applied for the purpose of forming an opinion on financial statements may bring instances of identified or suspected non-compliance to the auditor's attention. Maintaining professional skepticism throughout the audit, as required by ISA (UK) 200 (Revised June 2016),[3] is important in this context, given the extent of laws and regulations that affect the entity.

Effective Date

This ISA (UK) is effective for audits of financial statements for periods commencing on or   **9**
after 17 June 2016. Earlier adoption is permitted.

---

[2] *ISA (UK) 200 (Revised June 2016), paragraph A51.*

[3] *ISA (UK) 200 (Revised June 2016), paragraph 15.*

Objectives

10   The objectives of the auditor are:

(a) To obtain sufficient appropriate audit evidence regarding compliance with the provisions of those laws and regulations generally recognized to have a direct effect on the determination of material amounts and disclosures in the financial statements;

(b) To perform specified audit procedures to help identify instances of non-compliance with other laws and regulations that may have a material effect on the financial statements; and

(c) To respond appropriately to non-compliance or suspected non-compliance with laws and regulations identified during the audit.

Definition

11   For the purposes of this ISA (UK), the following term has the meaning attributed below:

Non-compliance – Acts of omission or commission by the entity, either intentional or unintentional, which are contrary to the prevailing laws or regulations. Such acts include transactions entered into by, or in the name of, the entity, or on its behalf, by those charged with governance, management or employees. Non-compliance does not include personal misconduct (unrelated to the business activities of the entity) by those charged with governance, management or employees of the entity.

11-1 This ISA (UK) also refers to 'money laundering'. 'Money laundering' is defined in legislation[3a] and in general terms involves an act which conceals, disguises, converts, transfers, removes, uses, acquires or possesses property resulting from criminal conduct.

Requirements

The Auditor's Consideration of Compliance with Laws and Regulations

12   As part of obtaining an understanding of the entity and its environment in accordance with ISA (UK) 315 (Revised June 2016),[4] the auditor shall obtain a general understanding of:

(a) The legal and regulatory framework applicable to the entity and the industry or sector in which the entity operates; and

(b) How the entity is complying with that framework. (Ref: Para. A7)

13   The auditor shall obtain sufficient appropriate audit evidence regarding compliance with the provisions of those laws and regulations generally recognized to have a direct effect on the determination of material amounts and disclosures in the financial statements. (Ref: Para. A8–A8-1)

14   The auditor shall perform the following audit procedures to help identify instances of non-compliance with other laws and regulations that may have a material effect on the financial statements: (Ref: Para. A9–A10-1)

[3a] *In the UK, the sMoney Laundering Regulations 2007 and the requirements of the Proceeds of Crime Act 2002 bring auditors within the regulated sector, requiring them to report suspected money laundering activity and adopt rigorous client identification procedures and appropriate anti-money laundering procedures.*

[4] ISA (UK) 315 (Revised June 2016), Identifying and Assessing the Risks of Material Misstatement through Understanding the Entity and Its Environment, *paragraph 11.*

(a) Inquiring of management and, where appropriate, those charged with governance, as to whether the entity is in compliance with such laws and regulations; and

(b) Inspecting correspondence, if any, with the relevant licensing or regulatory authorities.

During the audit, the auditor shall remain alert to the possibility that other audit procedures   **15**
applied may bring instances of non-compliance or suspected non-compliance with laws and regulations to the auditor's attention. (Ref: Para. A11–A11-2)

The auditor shall request management and, where appropriate, those charged with   **16**
governance to provide written representations that all known instances of non-compliance or suspected non-compliance with laws and regulations whose effects should be considered when preparing financial statements have been disclosed to the auditor. (Ref: Para. A12)

In the absence of identified or suspected non-compliance, the auditor is not required to   **17**
perform audit procedures regarding the entity's compliance with laws and regulations, other than those set out in paragraphs 12–16.

Audit Procedures When Non-Compliance Is Identified or Suspected

If the auditor becomes aware of information concerning an instance of non-compliance   **18**
or suspected non-compliance with laws and regulations, the auditor shall obtain: (Ref: Para. A13)

(a) An understanding of the nature of the act and the circumstances in which it has occurred; and

(b) Further information to evaluate the possible effect on the financial statements. (Ref: Para. A14)

If the auditor suspects there may be non-compliance, the auditor shall[4a] discuss the matter   **19**
with management and, where appropriate, those charged with governance. If management or, as appropriate, those charged with governance do not provide sufficient information that supports that the entity is in compliance with laws and regulations and, in the auditor's judgment, the effect of the suspected non-compliance may be material to the financial statements, the auditor shall consider the need to obtain legal advice. (Ref: Para. A15-A16)

If sufficient information about suspected non-compliance cannot be obtained, the auditor   **20**
shall evaluate the effect of the lack of sufficient appropriate audit evidence on the auditor's opinion.

The auditor shall evaluate the implications of non-compliance in relation to other aspects   **21**
of the audit, including the auditor's risk assessment and the reliability of written representations, and take appropriate action. (Ref: Para. A17–A18-1)

[4a] *Subject to compliance with legislation relating to 'tipping off'.*
In the UK, 'tipping off' is an offence under the Proceeds of Crime Act 2002 (POCA) Section 333A. It arises when an individual discloses:
(a) that a report (internal or external) has already been made where the disclosure by the individual is likely to prejudice an investigation which might be conducted following the internal or external report that has been made; or
(b) that an investigation is being contemplated or is being carried out into allegations that a money laundering offence has been committed and the disclosure by the individual is likely to prejudice that investigation.
Whilst "tipping off" requires a person to have knowledge or suspicion that a report has been or will be made, a further offence of prejudicing an investigation is included in POCA Section 342. Under this provision, it is an offence to make any disclosure which may prejudice an investigation of which a person has knowledge or suspicion, or to falsify, conceal, destroy or otherwise dispose of, or cause or permit the falsification, concealment, destruction or disposal of, documents relevant to such an investigation.
The disclosure offences under Sections 333A and 342 are not committed if the person disclosing does not know or suspect that it is likely to prejudice an investigation.

Reporting of Identified or Suspected Non-Compliance

Reporting Non-Compliance to Those Charged with Governance

22   Unless all of those charged with governance are involved in management of the entity, and therefore are aware of matters involving identified or suspected non-compliance already communicated by the auditor,[5] the auditor shall[4a] communicate with those charged with governance matters involving non-compliance with laws and regulations that come to the auditor's attention during the course of the audit, other than when the matters are clearly inconsequential.

22R-1   For audits of financial statements of public interest entities, when an auditor suspects or has reasonable grounds to suspect that irregularities, including fraud with regard to the financial statements of the entity, may occur or have occurred, the auditor shall, unless prohibited by law or regulation, inform the entity and invite it to investigate the matter and take appropriate measures to deal with such irregularities and to prevent any recurrence of such irregularities in the future. (Ref: Para. A18-2–A18-3)

23   If, in the auditor's judgment, the non-compliance referred to in paragraph 22 is believed to be intentional and material, the auditor shall[4a] communicate the matter to those charged with governance as soon as practicable. (Ref: Para. A18-4)

24   If the auditor suspects that management or those charged with governance are involved in non-compliance, the auditor shall[4a] communicate the matter to the next higher level of authority at the entity, if it exists, such as an audit committee or supervisory board. Where no higher authority exists, or if the auditor believes that the communication may not be acted upon or is unsure as to the person to whom to report, the auditor shall consider the need to obtain legal advice. (Ref: Para. A18-5)

Reporting Non-Compliance in the Auditor's Report on the Financial Statements

25   If the auditor concludes that the non-compliance has a material effect on the financial statements, and has not been adequately reflected in the financial statements, the auditor shall,[4a] in accordance with ISA (UK) 705 (Revised June 2016), express a qualified opinion or an adverse opinion on the financial statements.[6]

26   If the auditor is precluded by management or those charged with governance from obtaining sufficient appropriate audit evidence to evaluate whether non-compliance that may be material to the financial statements has, or is likely to have, occurred, the auditor shall[4a] express a qualified opinion or disclaim an opinion on the financial statements on the basis of a limitation on the scope of the audit in accordance with ISA (UK) 705 (Revised June 2016).

27   If the auditor is unable to determine whether non-compliance has occurred because of limitations imposed by the circumstances rather than by management or those charged with governance, the auditor shall evaluate the effect on the auditor's opinion in accordance with ISA (UK) 705 (Revised June 2016). (Ref: Para. A18-6)

---

[5] *ISA (UK) 260 (Revised June 2016)*, Communication with Those Charged with Governance, *paragraph 13*.

[6] *ISA (UK) 705 (Revised June 2016)*, Modifications to the Opinion in the Independent Auditor's Report, *paragraphs 7–8*.

Reporting Non-Compliance to Regulatory and Enforcement Authorities

If the auditor has identified or suspects non-compliance with laws and regulations, the   **28**
auditor shall determine whether the auditor has a responsibility to report the identified or
suspected non-compliance to parties outside the entity. (Ref: Para. A19–A20)

> For audits of financial statements of public interest entities, where the entity does   **28R-1**
> not investigate the matter referred to in paragraph 22R-1, the auditor shall inform the
> authorities responsible for investigating such irregularities. (Ref: Para. A19-13–A19-14)

Documentation

The auditor shall include in the audit documentation identified or suspected   **29**
noncompliance with laws and regulations and the results of discussion with management
and, where applicable, those charged with governance and other parties outside the entity.[7]
(Ref: Para. A21)

***

Application and Other Explanatory Material

Responsibility for Compliance with Laws and Regulations (Ref: Para. 3-8)

It is the responsibility of management, with the oversight of those charged with governance,   **A1**
to ensure that the entity's operations are conducted in accordance with laws and regulations.
Laws and regulations may affect an entity's financial statements in different ways: for
example, most directly, they may affect specific disclosures required of the entity in the
financial statements or they may prescribe the applicable financial reporting framework.
They may also establish certain legal rights and obligations of the entity, some of which
will be recognized in the entity's financial statements. In addition, laws and regulations
may impose penalties in cases of non-compliance.

The following are examples of the types of policies and procedures an entity may implement   **A2**
to assist in the prevention and detection of non-compliance with laws and regulations:

- Monitoring legal requirements and ensuring that operating procedures are designed
  to meet these requirements.
- Instituting and operating appropriate systems of internal control.
- Developing, publicizing and following a code of conduct.
- Ensuring employees are properly trained and understand the code of conduct.
- Monitoring compliance with the code of conduct and acting appropriately to discipline
  employees who fail to comply with it.
- Engaging legal advisors to assist in monitoring legal requirements.
- Maintaining a register of significant laws and regulations with which the entity has to
  comply within its particular industry and a record of complaints.

In larger entities, these policies and procedures may be supplemented by assigning
appropriate responsibilities to the following:

- An internal audit function.
- An audit committee.
- A compliance function.

---

[7] *ISA (UK) 230 (Revised June 2016)*, Audit Documentation, *paragraphs 8–11, and paragraph A6.*

A2-1   In the UK, in certain sectors or activities (for example financial services), there are detailed laws and regulations that specifically require directors to have systems to ensure compliance. Breaches of these laws and regulations could have a material effect on the financial statements.

A2-2   In the UK, it is the directors' responsibility to prepare financial statements that give a true and fair view of the state of affairs of a company or group and of its profit or loss for the financial year. Accordingly it is necessary, where possible non-compliance with law or regulations has occurred which may result in a material misstatement in the financial statements, for them to ensure that the matter is appropriately reflected and/or disclosed in the financial statements.

A2-3   In the UK, directors and officers of companies have responsibility to provide information required by the auditor, to which they have a legal right of access.[7a] Such legislation also provides that it is a criminal offence to give to the auditor information or explanations which are misleading, false or deceptive.

Responsibility of the Auditor

A3   Non-compliance by the entity with laws and regulations may result in a material misstatement of the financial statements. Detection of non-compliance, regardless of materiality, may affect other aspects of the audit including, for example, the auditor's consideration of the integrity of management or employees.

A4   Whether an act constitutes non-compliance with laws and regulations is a matter for legal determination, which is ordinarily beyond the auditor's professional competence to determine. Nevertheless, the auditor's training, experience and understanding of the entity and its industry or sector may provide a basis to recognize that some acts, coming to the auditor's attention, may constitute non-compliance with laws and regulations.

A5   In accordance with specific statutory requirements, the auditor may be specifically required to report, as part of the audit of the financial statements, on whether the entity complies with certain provisions of laws or regulations. In these circumstances, ISA (UK) 700 (Revised June 2016)[8] or ISA 800[9] deal with how these audit responsibilities are addressed in the auditor's report. Furthermore, where there are specific statutory reporting requirements, it may be necessary for the audit plan to include appropriate tests for compliance with these provisions of the laws and regulations.

Considerations Specific to Public Sector Entities

A6   In the public sector, there may be additional audit responsibilities with respect to the consideration of laws and regulations which may relate to the audit of financial statements or may extend to other aspects of the entity's operations.

[7a] *In the UK, under Section 499 of the Companies Act 2006.*

[8] *ISA (UK) 700 (Revised June 2016)*, Forming an Opinion and Reporting on Financial Statements, *paragraph 38.*

[9] *ISA 800* Special Considerations—Audits of Financial Statements Prepared in Accordance with Special Purpose Frameworks, *paragraph 11.*
ISA 800 has not been promulgated by the FRC for application in the UK.

The Auditor's Consideration of Compliance with Laws and Regulations

Obtaining an Understanding of the Legal and Regulatory Framework (Ref: Para. 12)

To obtain a general understanding of the legal and regulatory framework, and how the entity complies with that framework, the auditor may, for example: **A7**

- Use the auditor's existing understanding of the entity's industry, regulatory and other external factors;
- Update the understanding of those laws and regulations that directly determine the reported amounts and disclosures in the financial statements;
- Inquire of management as to other laws or regulations that may be expected to have a fundamental effect on the operations of the entity;
- Inquire of management concerning the entity's policies and procedures regarding compliance with laws and regulations; and
- Inquire of management regarding the policies or procedures adopted for identifying, evaluating and accounting for litigation claims.

Laws and Regulations Generally Recognized to Have a Direct Effect on the Determination of Material Amounts and Disclosures in the Financial Statements (Ref: Para. 13)

Certain laws and regulations are well-established, known to the entity and within the entity's industry or sector, and relevant to the entity's financial statements (as described in paragraph 6(a)). They could include those that relate to, for example: **A8**

- The form and content of financial statements;[9a]
- Industry-specific financial reporting issues;
- Accounting for transactions under government contracts; or
- The accrual or recognition of expenses for income tax or pension costs.

In the UK, these laws and regulations include:

- Those which determine the circumstances under which a company is prohibited from making a distribution except out of profits available for the purpose.[9b]
- Those laws which require auditors expressly to report non-compliance, such as the requirements relating to the maintenance of adequate accounting records[9c] or the disclosure of particulars of directors' remuneration in a company's financial statements.[9d]

Some provisions in those laws and regulations may be directly relevant to specific assertions in the financial statements (for example, the completeness of income tax provisions), while others may be directly relevant to the financial statements as a whole (for example, the required statements constituting a complete set of financial statements). The aim of the requirement in paragraph 13 is for the auditor to obtain sufficient appropriate audit evidence regarding the determination of amounts and disclosures in the financial statements in compliance with the relevant provisions of those laws and regulations.

[9a] *In the UK, under The Small Companies and Groups (Accounts and Directors' Report) Regulations 2008 (SI 2008-409) and The Large and Medium-sized Companies and Groups (Accounts and Reports) Regulations 2008 (SI 2008-410).*

[9b] *In the UK, under Section 830 of the Companies Act 2006.*

[9c] *In the UK, under Section 498 of the Companies Act 2006.*

[9d] *In the UK, under Section 497 of the Companies Act 2006.*

Non-compliance with other provisions of such laws and regulations and other laws and regulations may result in fines, litigation or other consequences for the entity, the costs of which may need to be provided for in the financial statements, but are not considered to have a direct effect on the financial statements as described in paragraph 6(a).

A8-1   In the UK, the auditor's responsibility to express an opinion on an entity's financial statements does not extend to determining whether the entity has complied in every respect with applicable tax legislation. The auditor needs to obtain sufficient appropriate evidence to give reasonable assurance that the amounts included in the financial statements in respect of taxation are not materially misstated. This will usually include making appropriate enquiries of those advising the entity on taxation matters (whether within the audit firm or elsewhere). If the auditor becomes aware that the entity has failed to comply with the requirements of tax legislation, the auditor considers whether to report the matter to parties outside the entity.

Procedures to Identify Instances of Non-Compliance – Other Laws and Regulations (Ref: Para. 14)

A9   Certain other laws and regulations may need particular attention by the auditor because they have a fundamental effect on the operations of the entity (as described in paragraph 6(b)). Non-compliance with laws and regulations that have a fundamental effect on the operations of the entity may cause the entity to cease operations, or call into question the entity's continuance as a going concern. For example, non-compliance with the requirements of the entity's license or other entitlement to perform its operations could have such an impact (for example, for a bank, non-compliance with capital or investment requirements).[9e] There are also many laws and regulations relating principally to the operating aspects of the entity that typically do not affect the financial statements and are not captured by the entity's information systems relevant to financial reporting.

A10   As the financial reporting consequences of other laws and regulations can vary depending on the entity's operations, the audit procedures required by paragraph 14 are directed to bringing to the auditor's attention instances of non-compliance with laws and regulations that may have a material effect on the financial statements.

A10-1   When determining the type of procedures necessary in a particular instance the auditor takes account of the particular entity concerned and the complexity of the regulations with which it is required to comply. In general, a small company which does not operate in a regulated area will require few specific procedures compared with a large multinational corporation carrying on complex, regulated business.

Non-Compliance Brought to the Auditor's Attention by Other Audit Procedures (Ref: Para. 15)

A11   Audit procedures applied to form an opinion on the financial statements may bring instances of non-compliance or suspected non-compliance with laws and regulations to the auditor's attention. For example, such audit procedures may include:

- Reading minutes;
- Inquiring of the entity's management and in-house legal counsel or external legal counsel concerning litigation, claims and assessments; and
- Performing substantive tests of details of classes of transactions, account balances or disclosures.

[9e] *Such requirements exist in the UK under the Financial Services and Markets Act 2000.*

In the UK, the auditor is alert for instances of possible or actual non-compliance with laws and regulations including those that might incur obligations for partners and staff in audit firms to report to a regulatory or other enforcement authority. See paragraphs A11-2 and A19-1–A19-12.   **A11-1**

Money Laundering Offences

Anti-money laundering legislation in the UK imposes a duty on the auditor to report suspected money laundering activity. There are similar laws and regulations relating to financing terrorist offences.[9f] The detailed legislation in both countries differs but the impact on the auditor can broadly be summarized as follows: **A11-2**

- Partners and staff in audit firms are required to report suspicions of conduct which would constitute a criminal offence which gives rise to direct or indirect benefit.
- Partners and staff in audit firms need to be alert to the dangers of 'tipping-off' in the UK, as this will constitute a criminal offence under the anti-money laundering legislation.[4a]

Further detail is set out in Practice Note 12 (Revised): Money Laundering – Guidance for auditors on UK legislation.

Written Representations (Ref: Para. 16)

Because the effect on financial statements of laws and regulations can vary considerably, written representations provide necessary audit evidence about management's knowledge of identified or suspected non-compliance with laws and regulations, whose effects may have a material effect on the financial statements. However, written representations do not provide sufficient appropriate audit evidence on their own and, accordingly, do not affect the nature and extent of other audit evidence that is to be obtained by the auditor.[10]   **A12**

Audit Procedures When Non-Compliance Is Identified or Suspected

Indications of Non-Compliance with Laws and Regulations (Ref: Para. 18)

If the auditor becomes aware of the existence of, or information about, the following matters, it may be an indication of non-compliance with laws and regulations: **A13**

- Investigations by regulatory organizations and government departments or payment of fines or penalties.
- Payments for unspecified services or loans to consultants, related parties, employees or government employees.
- Sales commissions or agent's fees that appear excessive in relation to those ordinarily paid by the entity or in its industry or to the services actually received.
- Purchasing at prices significantly above or below market price.
- Unusual payments in cash, purchases in the form of cashiers' cheques payable to bearer or transfers to numbered bank accounts.
- Unusual transactions with companies registered in tax havens.
- Payments for goods or services made other than to the country from which the goods or services originated.
- Payments without proper exchange control documentation.

[9f] *In the UK, the Terrorism Act 2000 contains reporting requirements for the laundering of terrorist funds which include any funds that are likely to be used for the financing of terrorism.*

[10] *ISA (UK) 580*, Written Representations, *paragraph 4.*

- Existence of an information system which fails, whether by design or by accident, to provide an adequate audit trail or sufficient evidence.
- Unauthorized transactions or improperly recorded transactions.
- Adverse media comment.

Matters Relevant to the Auditor's Evaluation (Ref: Para. 18(b))

A14   Matters relevant to the auditor's evaluation[10a] of the possible effect on the financial statements include:

- The potential financial consequences of non-compliance with laws and regulations on the financial statements including, for example, the imposition of fines, penalties, damages, threat of expropriation of assets,[10b] enforced discontinuation of operations, and litigation.
- Whether the potential financial consequences require disclosure.
- Whether the potential financial consequences are so serious as to call into question the fair presentation of the financial statements, or otherwise make the financial statements misleading.

Audit Procedures (Ref: Para. 19)

A15   The auditor may discuss the findings with those charged with governance where they may be able to provide additional audit evidence. For example, the auditor may confirm that those charged with governance have the same understanding of the facts and circumstances relevant to transactions or events that have led to the possibility of noncompliance with laws and regulations.

A16   If management or, as appropriate, those charged with governance do not provide sufficient information to the auditor that the entity is in fact in compliance with laws and regulations, the auditor may consider it appropriate to consult with the entity's in-house legal counsel or external legal counsel about the application of the laws and regulations to the circumstances, including the possibility of fraud, and the possible effects on the financial statements. If it is not considered appropriate to consult with the entity's legal counsel or if the auditor is not satisfied with the legal counsel's opinion, the auditor may consider it appropriate to consult the auditor's own legal counsel as to whether a contravention of a law or regulation is involved, the possible legal consequences, including the possibility of fraud, and what further action, if any, the auditor would take.

Evaluating the Implications of Non-Compliance (Ref: Para. 21)

A17   As required by paragraph 21, the auditor evaluates the implications of non-compliance in relation to other aspects of the audit, including the auditor's risk assessment and the reliability of written representations. The implications of particular instances of noncompliance identified by the auditor will depend on the relationship of the perpetration and concealment, if any, of the act to specific control activities and the level of management or employees involved, especially implications arising from the involvement of the highest authority within the entity.

[10a]   *ISA (UK) 620 (Revised June 2016),* Using the Work of an Auditor's Expert *applies if the auditor judges it necessary to obtain appropriate expert advice in connection with the evaluation of the possible effect of legal matters on the financial statements.*

[10b]   *In the UK, the Proceeds of Crime Act 2002 provides procedures to enable the authorities to confiscate in criminal proceedings or bring an action for civil recovery of assets which represent the benefits of criminal conduct.*

In exceptional cases, the auditor may consider whether withdrawal from the engagement, where withdrawal is possible under applicable law or regulation, is necessary when management or those charged with governance do not take the remedial action that the auditor considers appropriate in the circumstances, even when the non-compliance is not material to the financial statements. When deciding whether withdrawal from the engagement is necessary, the auditor may consider seeking legal advice. If withdrawal from the engagement is not possible, the auditor may consider alternative actions, including describing the non-compliance in an Other Matter(s) paragraph in the auditor's report.[11]   **A18**

Withdrawal from the engagement by the auditor is a step of last resort. It is normally preferable for the auditor to remain in office to fulfil the auditor's statutory duties, particularly where minority interests are involved. However, there are circumstances where there may be no alternative to withdrawal, for example where the directors of a company refuse to issue its financial statements or the auditor wishes to inform the shareholders or creditors of the company of the auditor's concerns and there is no immediate occasion to do so.   **A18-1**

Reporting of Identified or Suspected Non-Compliance

Reporting Non-Compliance to Those Charged with Governance
(Ref: Para. 22R-1-23)

For audits of financial statements of public interest entities, ISA (UK) 260 (Revised June 2016)[11a] requires the auditor to communicate in the additional report to the audit committee any significant matters involving actual or suspected non-compliance with laws and regulations or articles of association which were identified in the course of the audit.   **A18-2**

In the UK, laws or regulations may prohibit alerting ('tipping off') the entity when, for example, the auditor is required to report the non-compliance to an appropriate authority pursuant to anti-money laundering legislation.   **A18-3**

If a non-compliance is intentional but not material the auditor considers whether the nature and circumstances make it appropriate to communicate to those charged with governance as soon as practicable.   **A18-4**

Suspicion that Management or Those Charged with Governance are Involved in Non-Compliance (Ref: Para. 24)

In the case of suspected Money Laundering it may be appropriate to report the matter direct to the appropriate authority.   **A18-5**

---

[11] *ISA (UK) 706 (Revised June 2016), Emphasis of Matter Paragraphs and Other Matter Paragraphs in the Independent Auditor's Report, paragraph 8.*
In the UK, if the auditor concludes that the view given by the financial statements could be affected by a level of uncertainty concerning the consequences of a suspected or actual non-compliance which, in the auditor's opinion, is significant, the auditor, subject to a consideration of 'tipping off' (see footnote 4a), includes an explanatory paragraph referring to the matter in the auditor's report.

[11a] *ISA (UK) 260 (Revised June 2016), paragraph 16R-2(k).*

Reporting Non-Compliance in the Auditor's Report on the Financial Statements
(Ref: Para. 27)

A18-6   In the UK, when considering whether the financial statements reflect the possible consequences of any suspected or actual non-compliance, the auditor has regard to the requirements of applicable accounting standards. Suspected or actual non-compliance with laws or regulations may require disclosure in the financial statements because, although the immediate financial effect on the entity may not be material,[11b] there could be future material consequences such as fines or litigation. For example, an illegal payment may not itself be material but may result in criminal proceedings against the entity or loss of business which could have a material effect on the true and fair view given by the financial statements.

Reporting Non-Compliance to Regulatory and Enforcement Authorities (Ref: Para. 28)

A19   The auditor's professional duty to maintain the confidentiality of client information may preclude reporting identified or suspected non-compliance with laws and regulations to a party outside the entity. However, the auditor's legal responsibilities vary by jurisdiction and, in certain circumstances, the duty of confidentiality may be overridden by statute, the law or courts of law. In some jurisdictions, the auditor of a financial institution has a statutory duty to report the occurrence, or suspected occurrence, of non-compliance with laws and regulations to supervisory authorities. Also, in some jurisdictions, the auditor has a duty to report misstatements to authorities in those cases where management and, where applicable, those charged with governance fail to take corrective action. The auditor may consider it appropriate to obtain legal advice to determine the appropriate course of action.

A19-1   Legislation in the UK establishes specific responsibilities for the auditor to report suspicions regarding certain criminal offences (e.g., in relation to money laundering offences (see paragraph A11-2)). In addition, the auditor of entities subject to statutory regulation,[11c] has separate responsibilities to report certain information direct to the relevant regulator. Standards and guidance on these responsibilities is given in Section B of this ISA (UK) and relevant FRC Practice Notes.

A19-2   The procedures and guidance in Section B of this ISA (UK) can be adapted to circumstances in which the auditor of other types of entity becomes aware of a suspected instance of non-compliance with laws or regulations which the auditor is under a statutory duty to report.

Timing of Reports

A19-3   Some laws and regulations stipulate a period within which reports are to be made. If the auditor becomes aware of a suspected or actual non-compliance with law and regulations which gives rise to a statutory duty to report, the auditor complies with any such stipulated periods for reporting. Ordinarily the auditor makes a report to the appropriate authority as soon as practicable.

[11b] *As discussed in ISA (UK) 320 (Revised June 2016),* Materiality in Planning and Performing an Audit, *judgments about materiality are made in light of surrounding circumstances and are affected by the size or nature of a matter or a combination of both.*

[11c] *Auditors of public interest entities, financial service entities, pension schemes and charities have a statutory responsibility, subject to compliance with legislation relating to 'tipping off' (see footnote 4a), to report matters that are likely to be of material significance to the regulator.*

Reporting in the Public Interest

Where the auditor becomes aware of a suspected or actual instance of non-compliance   **A19-4**
with law or regulations which does not give rise to a statutory duty to report to an
appropriate authority the auditor considers whether the matter may be one that ought to
be reported to a proper authority in the public interest and, where this is the case, except
in the circumstances covered in paragraph A19-6 below, discusses the matter with those
charged with governance, including any audit committee.11d28

If, having considered any views expressed on behalf of the entity and in the light of   **A19-5**
any legal advice obtained, the auditor concludes that the matter ought to be reported to
an appropriate authority in the public interest, the auditor notifies those charged with
governance in writing of the view and, if the entity does not voluntarily do so itself or
is unable to provide evidence that the matter has been reported, the auditor reports it.

The auditor reports a matter direct to a proper authority in the public interest and without   **A19-6**
discussing the matter with the entity if the auditor concludes that the suspected or
actual instance of non-compliance has caused the auditor no longer to have confidence
in the integrity of those charged with governance.

Examples of circumstances which may cause the auditor no longer to have confidence   **A19-7**
in the integrity of those charged with governance include situations:

- Where the auditor suspects or has evidence of the involvement or intended
  involvement of those charged with governance in possible non-compliance with
  law or regulations which could have a material effect on the financial statements;
  or
- Where the auditor is aware that those charged with governance are aware of such
  non-compliance and, contrary to regulatory requirements or the public interest,
  have not reported it to a proper authority within a reasonable period. In such a
  case, if the auditor determines that continued holding of office is untenable or
  the auditor is removed from office by the client, the auditor will be mindful of
  the auditor's reporting duties.[11e]

Determination of where the balance of public interest lies requires careful consideration.   **A19-8**
An auditor whose suspicions have been aroused uses professional judgment to
determine whether the auditor's misgivings justify the auditor in carrying the matter
further or are too insubstantial to deserve reporting. The auditor is protected from the
risk of liability for breach of confidence or defamation provided that:

- In the case of breach of confidence, disclosure is made in the public interest,
  and such disclosure is made to an appropriate body or person,[11f] and there is no
  malice motivating the disclosure; and
- In the case of defamation disclosure is made in the auditor's capacity as auditor
  of the entity concerned, and there is no malice motivating the disclosure.

[11d] *In rare circumstances, according to common law, disclosure might also be justified in the public interest where
there is no instance of non-compliance with law or regulations, e.g. where the public is being misled or their
financial interests are being damaged; where a miscarriage of justice has occurred; where the health and safety of
members of the public or the environment is being endangered – although such events may well constitute breaches
of law or regulation.*

[11e] *In the UK, under Part 16 of the Companies Act 2006.*

[11f] *In the UK, proper authorities could include the Serious Fraud Office, the Crown Prosecution Service, police
forces, the Financial Services Authority the Panel on Takeovers and Mergers, the Society of Lloyd's, local authorities,
the Charity Commissioners for England and Wales, the Scottish Office For Scottish Charities, HM Revenue and
Customs, the Department of Business Innovation and Skills and the Health and Safety Executive.*

In addition, the auditor is protected from such risks where the auditor is expressly permitted or required by legislation to disclose information.[11g]

A19-9   'Public interest' is a concept that is not capable of general definition. Each situation must be considered individually. In the UK, legal precedent indicates that matters to be taken into account when considering whether disclosure is justified in the public interest may include:

- The extent to which the suspected or actual non-compliance with law or regulations is likely to affect members of the public;
- Whether those charged with governance have rectified the matter or are taking, or are likely to take, effective corrective action;
- The extent to which non-disclosure is likely to enable the suspected or actual noncompliance with law or regulations to recur with impunity;
- The gravity of the matter;
- Whether there is a general ethos within the entity of disregarding law or regulations; and
- The weight of evidence and the degree of the auditor's suspicion that there has been an instance of non-compliance with law or regulations.

A19-10   An auditor who can demonstrate having acted reasonably and in good faith in informing an authority of a breach of law or regulations which the auditor thinks has been committed would not be held by the court to be in breach of duty to the client even if, an investigation or prosecution having occurred, it were found that there had been no offence.

A19-11   The auditor needs to remember that the auditor's decision as to whether to report, and if so to whom, may be called into question at a future date, for example on the basis of:

- What the auditor knew at the time;
- What the auditor ought to have known in the course of the audit;
- What the auditor ought to have concluded; and
- What the auditor ought to have done.

The auditor may also wish to consider the possible consequences if financial loss is occasioned by non-compliance with law or regulations which the auditor suspects (or ought to suspect) has occurred but decided not to report.

A19-12   The auditor may need to take legal advice before making a decision on whether the matter needs to be reported to a proper authority in the public interest.

Reporting to Authorities of Public Interest Entities (Ref: Para. 28R-1)

A19-13   The disclosure in good faith to the authorities responsible for investigating such irregularities, by the auditor, of any irregularities referred to in paragraph 28R-1

[11g] *The Employments Rights Act 1996 in the UK would give similar protection to an individual member of the audit engagement team who made an appropriate report in the public interest. However, ordinarily a member of the engagement team who believed there was a reportable matter would follow the audit firm's policies and procedures to address such matters. ISA (UK) 220 (Revised June 2016),* Quality Control for an Audit of Financial Statements, *paragraph 18(a), requires that the engagement partner shall take responsibility for the engagement team undertaking appropriate consultation on difficult or contentious matters. If differences of opinion arise within the engagement team, ISA (UK) 220 (Revised June 2016), paragraph 22, requires that the engagement team shall follow the firm's policies and procedures for dealing with and resolving differences of opinion.*

shall not constitute a breach of any contractual or legal restriction on disclosure of information in accordance with the Audit Regulation.[11h]

The auditor considers whether to take further action when the entity investigates the matter referred to in paragraph 22R-1 but where the measures taken by management or those charged with governance, in the auditor's professional judgement, were not appropriate to deal with the irregularities identified or would fail to prevent future occurrences.   A19-14

Considerations Specific to Public Sector Entities

A public sector auditor may be obliged to report on instances of non-compliance to the legislature or other governing body or to report them in the auditor's report.   A20

Documentation (Ref: Para. 29)

The auditor's documentation of findings regarding identified or suspected non-compliance with laws and regulations may include, for example: A21

*   Copies of records or documents.
*   Minutes of discussions held with management, those charged with governance or parties outside the entity.

[11h] *Article 7 of Regulation (EU) No 537/2014 of the European Parliament and of the Council of 16 April 2014.*

International Standard on Auditing (UK) 250 (Revised June 2016)

Section B – The auditor's statutory right and duty to report to regulators of public interest entities and regulators of other entities in the financial sector

(Effective for audits of financial statements for periods commencing on or after 17 June 2016)

Contents

International Standard on Auditing (UK) (ISA (UK)) 250 (Revised June 2016), *Consideration of Laws and Regulations in an Audit of Financial Statements*, should be read in conjunction with ISA (UK) 200 (Revised June 2016), *Overall Objectives of the Independent Auditor and the Conduct of an Audit in Accordance with International Standards on Auditing (UK)*.

Introduction

Scope of this Section

This Section of ISA (UK) 250 deals with the circumstances in which the auditor of an entity subject to statutory regulation (a 'regulated entity') is required to report direct to a regulator information which comes to the auditor's attention in the course of the work undertaken in the auditor's capacity as auditor of the regulated entity. This may include work undertaken to express an opinion on the entity's financial statements, other financial information or on other matters specified by legislation or by a regulator. **1**

The Auditor's Responsibilities (Ref: Para. A1–A8)

The auditor of a regulated entity generally has special reporting responsibilities in addition to the responsibility to report on financial statements. These special reporting responsibilities take two forms: **2**

(a) *A responsibility to provide a report on matters specified in legislation or by a regulator.* This form of report is often made on an annual or other routine basis and does not derive from another set of reporting responsibilities. The auditor is required to carry out appropriate procedures sufficient to form an opinion on the matters concerned. These procedures may be in addition to those carried out to form an opinion on the financial statements; and

(b) *A statutory duty to report certain information, relevant to the regulators' functions, that come to the auditor's attention in the course of the audit work.* The auditor has no responsibility to carry out procedures to search out the information relevant to the regulator. This form of report is derivative in nature, arising only in the context of another set of reporting responsibilities, and is initiated by the auditor on discovery of a reportable matter.

This Section of this ISA (UK) deals with both forms of direct reports. Guidance on the auditor's responsibility to provide special reports on a routine basis on other matters specified in legislation or by a regulator is given in the Practice Notes dealing with regulated business, for example banks, building societies, investment businesses and insurers. **3**

The statutory duty to report to a regulator applies to information which comes to the attention of the auditor in the auditor's capacity as auditor. In determining whether information is obtained in that capacity, two criteria in particular need to be considered: first, whether the person who obtained the information also undertook the audit work; and if so, whether it was obtained in the course of or as a result of undertaking the audit work. Appendix 2 to this Section of this ISA (UK) sets out guidance on the application of these criteria. **4**

The auditor may have a statutory right to bring information to the attention of the regulator in particular circumstances which lie outside those giving rise to a statutory duty to initiate a direct report. Where this is so, the auditor may use that right to make a direct report relevant to the regulator on a specific matter which comes to the auditor's attention when the auditor concludes that doing so is necessary to protect the interests of those for whose benefit the regulator is required to act. **5**

The requirements and explanatory material in this section of this ISA (UK) complement but do not replace the legal and regulatory requirements applicable to each regulated entity. Where the application of those legal and regulatory requirements, taking into **6** account any published interpretations, is insufficiently clear for the auditor to determine whether a particular circumstance results in a legal duty to make a report to a regulator, or a right to make such a report, it may be appropriate to take legal advice.

Effective Date

7   This Section of ISA (UK) 250 (Revised June 2016) is effective for audits of financial statements for periods commencing on or after 17 June 2016. Earlier adoption is permitted.

Objective

8   The objective of the auditor of a regulated entity is to bring information of which the auditor has become aware in the ordinary course of performing work undertaken to fulfil the auditor's audit responsibilities to the attention of the appropriate regulator as soon as practicable when:

(a)   The auditor concludes that it is relevant to the regulator's functions having regard to such matters as may be specified in statute or any related regulations; and
(b)   In the auditor's opinion there is reasonable cause to believe it is or may be of material significance to the regulator.

Definitions

9   For purposes of this Section of this ISA (UK), the following terms have the meanings attributed below:

(a)   **The Act(s)** – Means those Acts that give rise to a duty to report to a regulator. For example, in the UK, this includes the Audit Regulation,[1] the Financial Services and Markets Act 2000, the Financial Services Act 2012 and regulations made under those Acts, and any future legislation including provisions relating to the duties of auditors similar to those contained in that statute.
(b)   **Audit** – For the purpose of this Section of this ISA (UK), the term 'audit' refers both to an engagement to report on the financial statements of a regulated entity and to an engagement to provide a report on other matters specified by statute or by a regulator undertaken in the capacity of auditor.
(c)   **Auditor** – The term 'auditor' should be interpreted in accordance with the requirements of the Acts. Guidance on its interpretation is contained in Practice Notes relating to each area of the financial sector to which the duty applies.
(d)   **Material significance** – The term 'material significance' requires interpretation in the context of the specific legislation applicable to the regulated entity. A matter or group of matters is normally of material significance to a regulator's functions when, due either to its nature or its potential financial impact, it is likely of itself to require investigation by the regulator. Further guidance on the interpretation of the term in the context of specific legislation is contained in Practice Notes dealing with the rights and duties of auditors of regulated entities to report direct to regulators.
(e)   **Regulated entity** – An individual, company or other type of entity which is:
   (i)   Authorized to carry on business in the financial sector which is subject to statutory regulation; or
   (ii)   A public interest entity.[2]

---

[1]   *Regulation (EU) No 537/2014 of the European Parliament and of the Council of 16 April 2014.*

[2]   *ISA (UK) 220 (Revised June 2016), Quality Control for an Audit of Financial Statements, paragraph 7(m)-1 defines public interest entity.*

(f) **Regulator** – Such persons as are empowered by the Act(s) to regulate the entity. The term includes the Financial Conduct Authority, the Prudential Regulation Authority, and such other bodies as may be so empowered in future legislation.

(g) 'Tipping off' – Involves a disclosure that is likely to prejudice any investigation into suspected money laundering which might arise from a report being made to a regulatory authority.[3] Money laundering involves an act which conceals, disguises, converts, transfers, removes, uses, acquires or possesses property which constitutes or represents a benefit from criminal conduct.

Requirements

Conduct of the Audit

Planning

When obtaining an understanding of the business for the purpose of the audit, the auditor of a regulated entity shall obtain an understanding of its current activities, the scope of its authorization and the effectiveness of its control environment. (Ref: Para. A9–A16)   **10**

Supervision and Control

The auditor shall ensure that all staff involved in the audit of a regulated entity have an understanding of: **11**

(a) The provisions of applicable legislation;
(b) The regulator's rules and any guidance issued by the regulator; and
(c) Any specific requirements which apply to the particular regulated entity,

appropriate to their role in the audit and sufficient (in the context of that role) to enable them to identify situations which may give reasonable cause to believe that a matter should be reported to the regulator. (Ref: Para. A17–A23)

Identifying Matters Requiring a Report Direct to Regulators

Where an apparent breach of statutory or regulatory requirements comes to the auditor's attention, the auditor shall: **12**

(a) Obtain such evidence as is available to assess its implications for the auditor's reporting responsibilities;
(b) Determine whether, in the auditor's opinion, there is reasonable cause to believe that the breach is of material significance to the regulator; and
(c) Consider whether the apparent breach is criminal conduct that gives rise to criminal property and, as such, should be reported to the specified authorities. (Ref: Para. A24–A30)

---

[3] *More detail is provided in the definition contained in Section A of ISA (UK) 250 (Revised June 2016).*

Reporting (Ref: Para. A31–A46)

The Auditor's Statutory Duty to Report Direct to Regulators

13 When the auditor concludes, after appropriate discussion and investigations, that a matter which has come to the auditor's attention gives rise to a statutory duty to make a report the auditor shall[4] bring the matter to the attention of the regulator as soon as practicable in a form and manner which will facilitate appropriate action by the regulator. When the initial report is made orally, the auditor shall make a contemporaneous written record of the oral report and shall confirm the matter in writing to the regulator. (Ref: Para. A31–A35)

13R-1 For audits of financial statements of public interest entities, the auditor shall:

(a) Report promptly to the regulator any information concerning that public interest entity of which the auditor has become aware while carrying out the audit and which may bring about any of the following:

    (i) A material breach of the laws, regulations or administrative provisions which lay down, where appropriate, the conditions governing authorization or which specifically govern pursuit of the activities of such public interest entity; or

    (ii) A material threat or doubt concerning the continuous functioning of the public interest entity; or

    (iii) A refusal to issue an audit opinion on the financial statements or the issuing of an adverse or qualified opinion.

(b) Report any information referred to in paragraph 13R-1(a)(i)–(iii) of which the auditor becomes aware in the course of carrying out the audit of an undertaking having close links[5] with the public interest entity for which they are also carrying out the audit.

14 When the matter giving rise to a statutory duty to make a report direct to a regulator casts doubt on the integrity of those charged with governance or their competence to conduct the business of the regulated entity, the auditor shall[4] make the report to the regulator as soon as practicable and without informing those charged with governance in advance. (Ref: Para. A35)

The Auditor's Right to Report Direct to Regulators

15 When a matter comes to the auditor's attention which the auditor concludes does not give rise to a statutory duty to report but nevertheless may be relevant to the regulator's exercise of its functions, the auditor shall[2]:

(a) Consider whether the matter should be brought to the attention of the regulator under the terms of the appropriate legal provisions enabling the auditor to report direct to the regulator; and, if so

(b) Advise those charged with governance that in the auditor's opinion the matter should be drawn to the regulators' attention.

---

[4] *In the UK, subject to compliance with legislation relating to 'tipping off'.*

[5] *'Close links' is defined in point (38) of Article 4(1) of Regulation (EU) No 575/2013 of the European Parliament and of the Council of 26 June 2013.*

Where the auditor is unable to obtain, within a reasonable period, adequate evidence that those charged with governance have properly informed the regulator of the matter, the auditor shall[4] make a report direct to the regulator as soon as practicable. (Ref: Para. A36–A37)

Contents of a Report Initiated by the Auditor

When making or confirming in writing a report direct to a regulator, the auditor shall: **16**

(a) State the name of the regulated entity concerned;
(b) State the statutory power under which the report is made;
(c) State that the report has been prepared in accordance with ISA (UK) 250, Section B—*The Auditor's Statutory Right and Duty to Report to Regulators of Public Interest Entities and Regulators of Other Entities in the Financial Sector*;
(d) Describe the context in which the report is given;
(e) Describe the matter giving rise to the report;
(f) Request the regulator to confirm that the report has been received; and
(g) State the name of the auditor, the date of the written report and, where appropriate, the date on which an oral report was made to the regulator and the name and title of the individual to whom the oral report was made. (Ref: Para. A38–A39)

Relationship With Other Reporting Responsibilities

When issuing a report expressing an opinion on a regulated entity's financial statements   **17**
or on other matters specified by legislation or a regulator, the auditor:

(a) Shall consider whether there are consequential reporting issues affecting the auditor's opinion which arise from any report previously made direct to the regulator in the course of the auditor's appointment; and
(b) Shall assess whether any matters encountered in the course of the audit indicate a need for a further direct report. (Ref: Para. A40–A43)

***

Application and Other Explanatory Material

The Auditor's Responsibilities (Ref: Para. 2–6)

Before accepting appointment, the auditor follows the procedures identified in the   **A1**
FRC's Ethical Standard and the ethical pronouncements and Audit Regulations issued by the auditor's relevant professional body.

In the case of regulated entities, the auditor would in particular obtain an understanding   **A2**
of the appropriate statutory and regulatory requirements and a preliminary knowledge of the management and operations of the entity, so as to enable the auditor to determine whether a level of knowledge of the business adequate to perform the audit can be obtained. The procedures carried out by the auditor in seeking to obtain this preliminary understanding may include discussion with the previous auditor and, in some circumstances, with the regulator.

On ceasing to hold office, the auditor may be required by statute or by regulation to   **A3**
make specific reports concerning the circumstances relating to that event, and would also follow the procedures identified in the ethical guidance issued by the relevant professional body.

A4   In addition, the auditor of a regulated entity would assess whether it is appropriate to bring any matters of which the auditor is then aware to the notice of the regulator. Under legislation in the UK, this may be done either before or after ceasing to hold office, as the auditor's statutory right to disclose to a regulator information obtained in the course of the auditor's appointment is not affected by the auditor's removal, resignation or otherwise ceasing to hold office.

A5   The duty to make a report direct to a regulator does not impose upon the auditor a duty to carry out specific work: it arises solely in the context of work carried out to fulfil other reporting responsibilities. Accordingly, no auditing procedures in addition to those carried out in the normal course of auditing the financial statements, or for the purpose of making any other specified report, are necessary for the fulfilment of the auditor's responsibilities.

A6   It will, however, be necessary for the auditor to take additional time in carrying out a financial statement audit or other engagement to assess whether matters which come to the auditor's attention should be included in a direct report and, where appropriate, to prepare and submit the report. These additional planning and follow-up procedures do not constitute an extension of the scope of the financial statement audit or of other work undertaken to provide a specified report relating to a regulated entity. They are necessary solely in order to understand and clarify the reporting responsibility and, where appropriate, to make a report.

A7   The circumstances in which the auditor is required by statute to make a report direct to a regulator include matters which are not considered as part of the audit of financial statements or of work undertaken to discharge other routine responsibilities. For example, the duty to report would apply to information of which the auditor became aware in the course of the auditor's work which is relevant to the Financial Conduct Authority's criteria for approved persons, although the auditor is not otherwise required to express an opinion on such matters. However, legislation imposing a duty to make reports direct to regulators does not require the auditor to change the scope of the audit work, nor does it place on the auditor an obligation to conduct the audit work in such a way that there is reasonable certainty that the auditor will discover all matters which regulators might consider as being of material significance. Therefore, whilst the auditor of a regulated entity is required to be alert to matters which may require a report, the auditor is not expected to be aware of all circumstances which, had the auditor known of them, would have led the auditor to make such a report. It is only when the auditor becomes aware of such a matter during the conduct of the normal audit work that the auditor has an obligation to determine whether a report to the regulator is required by statute or appropriate for other reasons.

A8   Similarly, the auditor is not responsible for reporting on a regulated entity's overall compliance with rules with which it is required to comply nor is the auditor required to conduct the audit work in such a way that there is reasonable certainty that the auditor will discover breaches. Nevertheless, breaches of rules with which a regulated entity is required to comply may have implications for the financial statements and, accordingly, the auditor of a regulated entity needs to consider whether any actual or contingent liabilities may have arisen from breaches of regulatory requirements. Breaches of a regulator's requirements may also have consequences for other matters on which the auditor of a regulated entity is required to express an opinion and, if such breaches represent criminal conduct, could give rise to the need to report to specified authorities.

Conduct of the Audit

Planning (Ref: Para. 10)

ISAs (UK) require the auditor to obtain an understanding of the entity and its environment.[6]

A9

In the context of a regulated entity, the auditor's understanding of its environment needs to extend to the applicable statutory provisions, the rules of the regulator concerned and any guidance issued by the regulator on the interpretation of those rules, together with other guidance issued by relevant authorities, including the FRC.

A10

The auditor is also required to identify and assess the risks of material misstatements to provide a basis for designing and performing further audit procedures.[7] In making such an assessment the auditor takes into account the control environment, including the entity's higher level procedures for complying with the requirements of its regulator. Such a review gives an indication of the extent to which the general atmosphere and controls in the regulated entity are conducive to compliance, for example through consideration of *inter alia:*

A11

- The adequacy of procedures and training to inform staff of the requirements of relevant legislation and the rules or other regulations of the regulator.
- The adequacy of procedures for authorization of transactions.
- Procedures for internal review of the entity's compliance with regulatory or other requirements.
- The authority of, and any resources available to, the compliance officer/Money Laundering Reporting Officer (MLRO).
- Procedures to ensure that possible breaches of requirements are investigated by an appropriate person and are brought to the attention of senior management.

In some areas of the financial sector, conducting business outside the scope of the entity's authorization is a serious regulatory breach, and therefore of material significance to the regulator. In addition, it may result in fines, suspension or loss of authorization.

A12

Where the auditor's review of the reporting entity's activities indicates that published guidance by the regulator may not be sufficiently precise to enable the auditor to identify circumstances in which it is necessary to initiate a report, the auditor would consider whether it is necessary to discuss the matters specified in legislation with the appropriate regulator with a view to reaching agreement on its interpretation.

A13

Similarly, where a group includes two or more companies separately regulated by different regulators, there may be a need to clarify the regulators' requirements in any overlapping areas of activity. However, the statutory duty to make a report as presently defined arises only in respect of the legal entity subject to regulation. Therefore the auditor of an unregulated company in a group that includes one or more other companies which are authorized by regulators would not have a duty to report matters to the regulators of those companies.

A14

---

[6] *ISA (UK) 315 (Revised June 2016), Identifying and Assessing the Risks of Material Misstatement through Understanding the Entity and Its Environment, paragraph 11.*

[7] *ISA (UK) 315 (Revised June 2016), paragraph 25.*

A15   When a regulated entity is subject to provisions of two or more regulators, the auditor needs to take account of the separate reporting requirements in planning and conducting the audit work. Arrangements may exist for one regulatory body to rely on financial monitoring being carried out by another body (the 'lead regulator') and where this is the case, routine reports by the regulated entity's auditor may be made to the lead regulator alone.

A16   However, the auditor's statutory duty to report cannot be discharged by reliance on the lead regulator informing others. Therefore, where the auditor concludes that a matter is of material significance to one regulator, the auditor needs to assess the need for separate reports informing each regulator of matters which the auditor concludes are or may be of material significance to it.

Supervision and Control (Ref: Para. 11)

A17   ISAs (UK) require the engagement partner to take responsibility for the direction, supervision and performance of the audit engagement in compliance with professional standards and applicable legal and regulatory requirements.[8] Consequently, in planning and conducting the audit of a regulated entity the auditor needs to ensure that staff are alert to the possibility that a report to its regulator may be required.

A18   Auditing firms also need to establish adequate procedures to ensure that any matters which are discovered in the course of or as a result of audit work and may give rise to a duty to report are brought to the attention of the engagement partner responsible for the audit on a timely basis.

A19   The right and duty to report to a regulator applies to information of which the auditor becomes aware in the auditor's capacity as such. They do not extend automatically to any information obtained by a firm regardless of its source. Consequently partners and staff undertaking work in another capacity are not required to have detailed knowledge of the regulator's requirements (unless necessary for that other work) nor to bring information to the attention of the engagement partner responsible for the audit on a routine basis.

A20   However, as discussed further in Appendix 2, firms need to establish lines of communications, commensurate with their size and complexity, sufficient to ensure that non-audit work undertaken for a regulated entity which is likely to have an effect on the audit is brought to the attention of the engagement partner responsible for the audit, who will need to determine whether the results of non-audit work undertaken for a regulated entity ought to be assessed as part of the audit process.

Use of the Work of Other Auditors

A21   An auditor with responsibilities for reporting on financial statements including financial information of one or more components audited by other auditors is required to obtain sufficient appropriate audit evidence that the work of the other auditors is adequate for the purposes of the audit. The same principle applies to using the work of another auditor in a different type of engagement. The auditor of a regulated entity who uses the work undertaken by other auditors needs to establish reporting arrangements such that the other auditors bring to the attention of the auditor of the regulated entity matters arising from their work which may give rise to a duty to report to a regulator.

---

[8]   *ISA (UK) 220 (Revised June 2016), Quality Control for an Audit of Financial Statements, paragraph 15.*

The nature of the reporting arrangements will depend on the nature of the work   **A22**
undertaken by the other auditors. For example, the statutory duty to make a report
relates to the legal entity subject to regulation rather than to the entire group to which
that entity may belong. Consequently, the auditor of a holding company authorized
by one regulator would not be expected to have knowledge of all matters which come
to the attention of a component auditor. The auditor of the regulated entity would,
however, have a duty to report, where appropriate, matters which arise from the audit of
the regulated entity's own financial statements and of the consolidated group figures.

Where the audit of a regulated entity is undertaken by joint auditors, knowledge obtained   **A23**
by one firm is likely to be deemed to be known by the other. Care will therefore be
needed in agreeing and implementing arrangements to exchange information relating
to matters which may give rise to a duty to report to a regulator.

Identifying Matters Requiring a Report Direct to Regulators (Ref: Para. 12)

The precise matters which give rise to a statutory duty on auditors to make a report to   **A24**
a regulator derive from the relevant Acts. Broadly, such matters fall into three general
categories:

(a) The financial position of the regulated entity;
(b) Its compliance with requirements for the management of its business; and
(c) The status of those charged with governance as fit and proper persons.

Further detailed guidance on the interpretation of these matters in the context of
specific legislation applicable to each type of regulated entity is contained in Practice
Notes dealing with the rights and duties of auditors of regulated entities to report direct
to regulators.

In assessing the effect of an apparent breach, the auditor takes into account the quantity   **A25**
and type of evidence concerning such a matter which may reasonably be expected to be
available. If the auditor concludes that the auditor has been prevented from obtaining all
such evidence concerning a matter which may give rise to a duty to report, the auditor
would normally make a report direct to the regulator as soon as practicable.

An apparent breach of statutory or regulatory requirements may not of itself give rise to   **A26**
a statutory duty to make a report to a regulator. There will normally be a need for some
further investigation and discussion of the circumstances surrounding the apparent
breach with the directors in order to obtain sufficient information to determine whether
it points to a matter which is or may be of material significance to the regulator. For
example, a minor breach which has been corrected by the regulated entity and reported
(if appropriate) to the regulator, and which from the evidence available to the auditor
appears to be an isolated occurrence, would not normally give the auditor reasonable
cause to believe that it is or may be of material significance to the regulator. However,
a minor breach that results in a criminal offence that gave rise to the criminal property
would be reportable to the specified authorities under the anti-money laundering
legislation.

When determining whether a breach of statutory or regulatory requirements gives rise   **A27**
to a statutory duty to make a report direct to a regulator, the auditor considers factors
such as:

●   Whether the breach, though minor, is indicative of a general lack of compliance
    with the regulator's requirements or otherwise casts doubt on the status of those
    charged with governance as fit and proper persons.

- Whether a breach which occurred before the auditor's visit to the regulated entity was reported by the entity itself and has since been corrected, such that, at the date of the auditor's discovery, no breach exists.
- Whether the circumstances giving rise to a breach which occurred before the auditors visit to the regulated entity continue to exist, or those charged with governance have not taken corrective action, or the breach has re-occurred.
- Whether the circumstances suggest that an immediate report to the regulator is necessary in order to protect the interests of depositors, investors, policyholders, clients of the entity or others in whose interests the regulator is required to act.

A28   The auditor would normally seek evidence to assess the implications of a suspected breach before reporting a matter to the regulator. However, the auditor's responsibility to make a report does not require the auditor to determine the full implications of a matter before reporting: the auditor is required to exercise professional judgment as to whether or not there is reasonable cause to believe that a matter is or may be of material significance to the regulator. In forming that judgment, the auditor undertakes appropriate investigations to determine the circumstances but does not require the degree of evidence which would be a normal part of forming an opinion on financial statements. Such investigations would normally include:

- Enquiry of appropriate level of staff;
- Review of correspondence and documents relating to the transaction or event concerned; and
- Discussion with those charged with governance, or other senior management where appropriate.

In the case of a life company, it would also be appropriate to consult with the appointed actuary, who also has various statutory duties under insurance companies legislation.

A29   The potential gravity of some apparent breaches may be such that an immediate report to the regulator is essential in order to enable the regulator to take appropriate action: in particular, prompt reporting of a loss of client assets may be necessary to avoid further loss to investors or others in whose interests the regulator is required to act. The auditor is therefore required to balance the need for further investigation of the matter with the need for prompt reporting.

A30   On completion of the auditor's investigations, the auditor needs to ensure that the facts and the basis for the auditor's decision (whether to report or not) is adequately documented such that the reasons for that decision may be clearly demonstrated should the need to do so arise in future.

Reporting

The Auditor's Statutory Duty to Report Direct to Regulators (Ref: Para. 13–14)

A31   Except in the circumstances referred to in paragraph 14 the auditor seeks to reach agreement with those charged with governance on the circumstances giving rise to a report direct to the regulator. However, where a statutory duty to report arises, the auditor is required to make such a report regardless of:

(a) Whether the matter has been referred to the regulator by other parties (including the company, whether by those charged with governance or otherwise); and
(b) Any duty owed to other parties, including those charged with governance of the regulated entity and its shareholders (or equivalent persons).

Except in the circumstances set out in paragraph 14, the auditor sends a copy of the auditor's written report to those charged with governance and (where appropriate) audit committee of the regulated entity.   **A32**

In normal circumstances, the auditor would wish to communicate with the regulator with the knowledge and agreement of those charged with governance of the regulated entity. However, in some circumstances immediate notification of the discovery of a matter giving reasonable grounds to believe that a reportable matter exists will be necessary – for example, a phone call to alert the regulator followed by a meeting to discuss the circumstances.   **A33**

Speed of reporting is essential where the circumstances cause the auditor no longer to have confidence in the integrity of those charged with governance. In such circumstances, there may be a serious and immediate threat to the interests of depositors or other persons for whose protection the regulator is required to act; for example where the auditor believes that a fraud or other irregularity may have been committed by, or with the knowledge of, those charged with governance, or have evidence of the intention of those charged with governance to commit or condone a suspected fraud or other irregularity.   **A34**

In circumstances where the auditor no longer has confidence in the integrity of those charged with governance, it is not appropriate to provide those charged with governance with copies of the auditor's report. Since such circumstances will be exceptional and extreme, the auditor may wish to seek legal advice as to the auditor's responsibilities and the appropriate course of action.   **A35**

The Auditor's Right to Report Direct to Regulators (Ref: Para. 15)

The auditor may become aware of matters which the auditor concludes are relevant to the exercise of the regulator's functions even though they fall outside the statutory definition of matters which must be reported to a regulator. In such circumstances, the Acts in the UK provide the auditor with protection for making disclosure of the matter to the appropriate regulator.   **A36**

Where the auditor considers that a matter which does not give rise to a statutory duty to report is nevertheless, in the auditor's professional judgment, such that it should be brought to the attention of the regulator, it is normally appropriate for the auditor to request those charged with governance of the regulated entity in writing to draw it to the attention of the regulator.   **A37**

Contents of a Report Initiated by the Auditor (Ref: Para. 16)

Such a report is a by-product of other work undertaken by the auditor. As a result it is not possible for the auditor or the regulator to conclude that all matters relevant to the regulator were encountered in the course of the auditor's work. The auditor's report therefore sets out the context in which the information reported was identified and indicates the extent to which the matter has been investigated and discussed with those charged with governance.   **A38**

Matters to which the auditor may wish to refer when describing the context in which a report is made direct to a regulator include: **A39**

- The nature of the appointment from which the report derives. For example, it may be appropriate to distinguish between a report made in the course of an audit of financial statements and one which arises in the course of a more limited engagement, such as an appointment to report on specified matters by the Financial Conduct Authority;

- The applicable legislative requirements and interpretations of those requirements which have informed the auditor's judgment;
- The extent to which the auditor has investigated the circumstances giving rise to the matter reported;
- Whether the matter reported has been discussed with those charged with governance;
- Whether steps to rectify the matter have been taken.

Relationship With Other Reporting Responsibilities (Ref: Para. 17)

A40   The circumstances which give rise to a report direct to a regulator may involve an uncertainty or other matter which requires disclosure in the financial statements. The auditor will therefore need to consider whether the disclosures made in the financial statements are adequate for the purposes of giving a true and fair view of the regulated entity's state of affairs and profit or loss. Where the auditor considers it necessary to draw users' attention to a matter presented or disclosed in the financial statements that, in the auditor's judgment, is of such importance that it is fundamental to users' understanding of the financial statements, the auditor is required to include an Emphasis of Matter paragraph in the auditor's report.[9]

A41   Similarly, circumstances giving rise to a report direct to a regulator may also require reflection in the auditor's reports on other matters required by legislation or another regulator.

A42   In fulfilling the responsibility to report direct to a regulator, it is important that the auditor not only assess the significance of individual transactions or events but also consider whether a combination of such items over the course of the work undertaken for the auditor's primary reporting responsibilities may give the auditor reasonable grounds to believe that they constitute a matter of material significance to the regulator, and so give rise to a statutory duty to make a report.

A43   As there is no requirement for the auditor to extend the scope of the audit work to search for matters which may give rise to a statutory duty to report, such an assessment of the cumulative effect of evidence obtained in the course of an audit would be made when reviewing the evidence in support of the opinions to be expressed in the reports the auditor has been appointed to make. Where such a review leads to the conclusion that the cumulative effect of matters noted in the course of the audit is of material significance to the regulator, it will be appropriate for a report to be made as set out in paragraph 16. However, reports indicating a 'nil return' are not appropriate.

Communication of Information by the Regulator

A44   The Acts provide that, in certain exceptional circumstances, regulators may pass confidential information to another party. The precise circumstances in which regulators may disclose information varies, but in general they may do so if considered necessary to fulfil their own obligations under the appropriate Act, or, in some cases, to enable the auditor to fulfil the auditor's duties either to the

---

[9] ISA (UK) 706 (Revised June 2016), Emphasis of Matter Paragraphs and Other Matter Paragraphs in the Independent Auditor's Report, paragraph 6.

regulated entity or, in other cases, to the regulator. Confidential information remains confidential in the hands of the recipient.

In so far as the law permits, regulators have confirmed that they will consider taking the initiative in bringing a matter to the attention of the auditor of a regulated entity in circumstances where: **A45**

(a) They believe the matter is of such importance that the auditor's knowledge of it could significantly affect the form of the auditor's report on the entity's financial statements or other matters on which the auditor is required to report, or the way in which the auditor discharges the auditor's reporting responsibilities; and

(b) The disclosure is for the purpose of enabling or assisting the regulator to discharge its functions under the Acts.

The auditor needs to be aware that there may be circumstances in which the regulators are unable to disclose such information. Where the auditor of a regulated entity is not informed by the regulator of any matter, therefore, the auditor cannot assume that there are no matters known to the regulator which could affect the auditor's judgment as to whether information is of material significance. However, in the absence of disclosure by the regulator, the auditor can only form a judgment in the light of evidence to which the auditor has access. **A46**

For audits of public interest entities, the Audit Regulation[10] requires an effective dialogue to be established between the supervising credit institutions and insurance undertakings, on the one hand, and the auditor carrying out the audit of those institutions and undertakings, on the other hand. The responsibility for compliance with this requirement of the Audit Regulation rests with both parties to the dialogue. **A47**

---

[10] *Regulation (EU) No 537/2014 of the European Parliament and of the Council of 16 April 2014.*

Appendix 1

The Regulatory Framework in the Financial Sector

1   In the UK, legislation exists in the principal areas of financial services to protect the interests of investors, depositors in banks and other users of financial services. Regulated entities operating in the financial sector are required to comply with legal and regulatory requirements concerning the way their business is conducted. Compliance with those rules is monitored in four principal ways:

- Internal monitoring by those charged with governance of the regulated entity;
- Submission of regular returns by the regulated entity to the regulator;
- Monitoring and, in some cases, inspection of the entity by the regulator;
- Reports[4] by the reporting entity's auditor on its financial statements and other specified matters required by legislation or by the regulator.

Responsibility for Ensuring Compliance

2   Ensuring compliance with the requirements with which a regulated entity is required to comply in carrying out its business is the responsibility of those charged with governance of a regulated entity. It requires adequate organization and systems of controls. The regulatory framework provides that adequate procedures for compliance must be established and maintained. Those charged with governance of a regulated entity are also normally required to undertake regular reviews of compliance and to inform the regulator of any breach of the rules and regulations applicable to its regulated business. In addition, regulators may undertake compliance visits.

3   The auditor of a regulated entity normally has responsibilities for reporting[4] on particular aspects of its compliance with the regulator's requirements. However, the auditor has no direct responsibility for expressing an opinion on an entity's overall compliance with the requirements for the conduct of its business, nor does an audit provide any assurance that breaches of requirements which are not the subject of regular auditors' reports will be detected.

The Role of Auditors

4   Those charged with governance of regulated entities have primary responsibility for ensuring that all appropriate information is made available to regulators. Normal reporting procedures (including auditor's reports on records, systems and returns, and regular meetings with those charged with governance and/or management and auditors) supplemented by any inspection visits considered necessary by the regulators should provide the regulators with all the information they need to carry out their responsibilities under the relevant Act.

Routine Reporting by Auditors

5   Regulators' requirements for reports by auditors vary. In general terms, however, such reports may include opinions on:

- The regulated entity's annual financial statements;
- The regulated entity's compliance with requirements for financial resources; and

- The adequacy of the regulated entity's system of controls over its transactions and in particular over its clients' money and other property.

As a result of performing the work necessary to discharge their routine reporting responsibilities, or those arising from an appointment to provide a special report required by the regulator, the auditor of a regulated entity may become aware of matters which the auditor considers need to be brought to the regulator's attention sooner than would be achieved by routine reports by the entity or its auditor.

6

The auditor of a regulated entity normally has a right to communicate in good faith[4] information the auditor considers is relevant to the regulators' functions.

7

The Auditor's Statutory Duty to Report to the Regulator

In addition, the auditor is required by law to report[4] direct to a regulator when the auditor concludes that there is reasonable cause to believe that a matter is or may be of material significance to the regulator. The precise matters which result in a statutory duty to make such a report vary, depending upon the specific requirements of relevant legislation and the regulator's rules. In general, however, a duty to report to a regulator arises when the auditor becomes aware that:

8

- The regulated entity is in serious breach of:
  - ○ Requirements to maintain adequate financial resources; or
  - ○ Requirements for those charged with governance to conduct its business in a sound and prudent manner (including the maintenance of systems of control over transactions and over any clients' assets held by the business); or
- There are circumstances which give reason to doubt the status of those charged with governance or senior management as fit and proper persons.

Confidentiality

Confidentiality is an implied term of the auditor's contracts with client entities. However, in the circumstances leading to a right or duty to report,[4] the auditor is entitled to communicate to regulators in good faith information or opinions relating to the business or affairs of the entity or any associated body without contravening the duty of confidence owed to the entity and, in the case of a bank, building society and friendly society, its associated bodies.

9

The statutory provisions permitting the auditor to communicate information to regulators relate to information obtained in the auditor's capacity as auditor of the regulated entity concerned. Auditors and regulators therefore should be aware that confidential information obtained in other capacities may not normally be disclosed to another party.

10

Appendix 2   (Ref: Para. 4)

The Application of the Statutory Duty to Report to Regulators

Introduction

1   The statutory duty to report to a regulator[4] applies to information which comes to the attention of the auditor in the auditor's capacity as auditor. However, neither the term 'auditor' nor the phrase 'in the capacity of auditor' are defined in the legislation, nor has the court determined how these expressions should be construed.

2   As a result, it is not always clearly apparent when a firm should regard itself as having a duty to report to a regulator. For example, information about a regulated entity may be obtained when partners or staff of the firm which is appointed as its auditor carry out work for another client entity; or when the firm undertakes other work for the regulated entity. Auditors, regulated entities and regulators need to be clear as to when the normal duty of confidentiality will be overridden by the auditor's statutory duty to report to the regulator.

3   In order to clarify whether or not a firm should regard itself as bound by the duty, the FRC developed, in conjunction with HM Treasury and the regulators, guidance on the interpretation of the key conditions for the existence of that duty, namely that the firm is to be regarded as auditor of a regulated entity and that information is obtained in the capacity of auditor.

4   Guidance on the interpretation of the term 'auditor' in the context of each Act is contained in the separate Practice Notes dealing with each area affected by the legislation.

5   This appendix sets out guidance on the interpretation of the phrase 'in the capacity of auditor'. The Board nevertheless continues to hold the view that the meaning of the phrase should be clarified in legislation in the longer term.

In the Capacity of Auditor

6   In determining whether information is obtained in the capacity of auditor, two criteria in particular should be considered:

(a) Whether the person who obtained the information also undertook the audit work; and if so
(b) Whether it was obtained in the course of or as a result of undertaking the audit work.

7   It is then necessary to apply these criteria to information about a regulated entity which may become known from a number of sources, and by a number of different individuals within a firm. Within a large firm, for example, information may come to the attention of the partner responsible for the audit of a regulated entity, a partner in another office who undertakes a different type of work, or members of the firm's staff at any level. In the case of a sole practitioner who is the auditor of a regulated entity, information about a regulated entity may also be obtained by the practitioner in the course of work other than its audit.

Non-Audit Work Carried out in Relation to a Regulated Entity

Where partners or staff involved in the audit of a regulated entity carry out work   **8**
other than its audit (non-audit work) information about the regulated entity will be
known to them as individuals. In circumstances which suggest that a matter would
otherwise give rise to a statutory duty to report[4] if obtained in the capacity of auditor, it
will be prudent for them to make enquiries in the course of their audit work in order to
establish whether this is the case from information obtained in that capacity.

However, where non-audit work is carried out by other partners or staff, neither of the   **9**
criteria set out in paragraph 6 is met in respect of information which becomes known
to them. Nevertheless the firm should take proper account of such information when it
could affect the audit so that it is treated in a responsible manner, particularly since in
partnership law the knowledge obtained by one partner in the course of the partnership
business may be imputed to the entire partnership. In doing so, two types of work
may be distinguished: first, work which could affect the firm's work as auditor and,
secondly, work which is undertaken purely in an advisory capacity.

A firm appointed as auditor of a regulated entity needs to have in place appropriate   **10**
procedures to ensure that the partner responsible for the audit function is made aware
of any other relationship which exists between any department of the firm and the
regulated entity when that relationship could affect the firm's work as auditor. Common
examples of such work include accounting work, particularly for smaller entities, and
provision of tax services to the regulated entity.

Prima facie, information obtained in the course of non-audit work is not covered by   **11**
either the right or the duty to report to a regulator. However, the firm appointed as
auditor needs to consider whether the results of other work undertaken for a regulated
entity need to be assessed as part of the audit process. In principle, this is no different
to seeking to review a report prepared by outside consultants on, say, the entity's
accounting systems so as to ensure that the auditor makes a proper assessment of the
risks of misstatement in the financial statements and of the work needed to form an
opinion. Consequently, the partner responsible for the audit needs to make appropriate
enquiries in the process of planning and completing the audit (see paragraph 17 above).
Such enquiries would be directed to those aspects of the non-audit work which might
reasonably be expected to be relevant to the audit. When, as a result of such enquiries,
those involved in the audit become aware of issues which may be of material significance
to a regulator such issues should be considered, and if appropriate reported[4] following
the requirements set out in this Section of this ISA (UK).

Work which is undertaken in an advisory capacity, for example to assist the directors   **12**
of a regulated entity to determine effective and efficient methods of discharging their
duties, would not normally affect the work undertaken for the audit. Nevertheless, in
rare instances, the partner responsible for such advisory work may conclude that steps
considered necessary in order to comply with the regulator's requirements have not
been taken by the directors or that the directors intend in some respect not to comply
with the regulator's requirements. Such circumstances would require consideration in
the course of work undertaken for the audit, both to consider the effect on the auditor's
routine reports and to determine whether the possible non-compliance is or is likely to
be of material significance to the regulator.

Work Relating to a Separate Entity

13   Information obtained in the course of work relating to another entity audited by the same firm (or the same practitioner) is confidential to that other entity. The auditor is not required, and has no right, to report to a regulator confidential information which arises from work undertaken by the same auditing firm for another client. However, as a matter of sound practice, individuals involved in the audit of a regulated entity who become aware (in a capacity other than that of auditor of a regulated entity) of a matter which could otherwise give rise to a statutory duty to report would normally make enquiries in the course of their audit of the regulated entity to establish whether the information concerned is substantiated.

14   In carrying out the audit work, the auditor is required to have due regard to whether disclosure of non-compliance with laws and regulations to a proper authority is appropriate in the public interest. standards and guidance on this general professional obligation is set out in Section A of this ISA (UK).

Conclusion

15   The phrase 'in his capacity as auditor' limits information subject to the duty to report to matters of which the auditor becomes aware in the auditor's capacity as such. Consequently, it is unlikely that a partnership can be said to be acting in its capacity as auditor of a particular regulated entity whenever any apparently unrelated material comes to the attention of a partner or member of staff not engaged in that audit, particularly if that material is confidential to another client.

16   The statutory duty to report to a regulator[4] therefore does not extend automatically to any information obtained by a firm regardless of its source. Firms undertaking audits of regulated entities need, however, to establish lines of communication, commensurate with their size and organizational structure, sufficient to ensure that non-audit work undertaken for a regulated entity which is likely to have an effect on the audit is brought to the attention of the partner responsible for the audit and to establish procedures for the partner responsible for the audit to make appropriate enquiries of those conducting such other work as part of the process of planning and completing the audit.

Appendix 3

Action by the Auditor on Discovery of a Breach of a Regulator's Requirements

1   This appendix sets out in the form of a flowchart the steps involved in assessing whether a report to a regulator is required when a breach of the regulator's requirements comes to the attention of the auditor.

2   The flowchart is intended to provide guidance to readers in understanding this Section of this ISA (UK). It does not form part of the auditing standards contained in the ISA (UK).

Action by the Auditor on Discovery of a Breach of a Regulator's Requirement

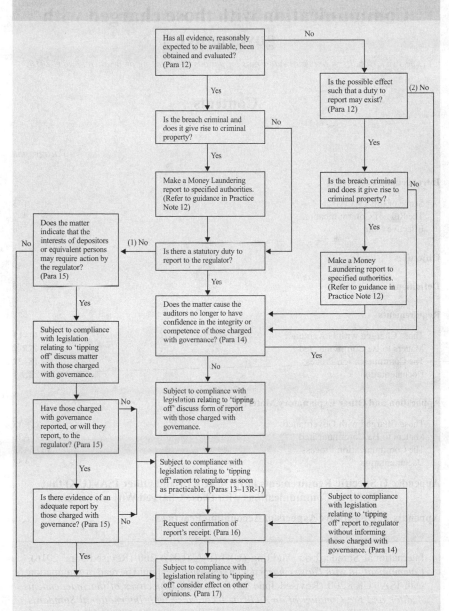

(1) This route would be only followed when a distinct right to report to the regulator exists. Otherwise, where no duty to report exists, the auditor would next consider the effect on other opinions.

(2) Where the auditor considers that a distinct right to report to the regulator exists, the auditor would next consider the question marked (1).

International Standard on Auditing (UK) 260 (Revised June 2016)

Communication with those charged with governance

(Effective for audits of financial statements for periods commencing on or after 17 June 2016)

Contents

International Standard on Auditing (UK) (ISA (UK)) 260 (Revised June 2016), *Communication with Those Charged with Governance*, should be read in conjunction with ISA (UK) 200 (Revised June 2016), *Overall Objectives of the Independent Auditor and the Conduct of an Audit in Accordance with International Standards on Auditing (UK)*.

Introduction

Scope of this ISA (UK)

This International Standard on Auditing (UK) (ISA (UK)) deals with the auditor's 1
responsibility to communicate with those charged with governance in an audit of financial
statements. Although this ISA (UK) applies irrespective of an entity's governance structure
or size, particular considerations apply where all of those charged with governance are
involved in managing an entity, and for listed entities. This ISA (UK) does not establish
requirements regarding the auditor's communication with an entity's management or
owners unless they are also charged with a governance role.

This ISA (UK) is written in the context of an audit of financial statements, but may also be 2
applicable, adapted as necessary in the circumstances, to audits of other historical financial
information when those charged with governance have a responsibility to oversee the
preparation of the other historical financial information.

Recognizing the importance of effective two-way communication in an audit of 3
financial statements, this ISA (UK) provides an overarching framework for the auditor's
communication with those charged with governance, and identifies some specific matters to
be communicated with them. Additional matters to be communicated, which complement
the requirements of this ISA (UK), are identified in other ISAs (UK) (see Appendix 1). In
addition, ISA (UK) 265[1] establishes specific requirements regarding the communication
of significant deficiencies in internal control the auditor has identified during the audit to
those charged with governance. Further matters, not required by this or other ISAs (UK),
may be required to be communicated by law or regulation, by agreement with the entity,
or by additional requirements applicable to the engagement, for example, the standards
of a national professional accountancy body. Nothing in this ISA (UK) precludes the
auditor from communicating any other matters to those charged with governance.
(Ref: Para. A33–A36)

The Role of Communication

This ISA (UK) focuses primarily on communications from the auditor to those charged 4
with governance. Nevertheless, effective two-way communication is important in assisting:

(a) The auditor and those charged with governance in understanding matters related
to the audit in context, and in developing a constructive working relationship.
This relationship is developed while maintaining the auditor's independence and
objectivity;
(b) The auditor in obtaining from those charged with governance information relevant
to the audit.[1a] For example, those charged with governance may assist the auditor in
understanding the entity and its environment, in identifying appropriate sources of
audit evidence, and in providing information about specific transactions or events;
and
(c) Those charged with governance in fulfilling their responsibility to oversee the
financial reporting process, thereby reducing the risks of material misstatement of the
financial statements.

---

[1] *ISA (UK) 265*, Communicating Deficiencies in Internal Control to Those Charged with Governance and
Management.

[1a] *In the UK, Sections 499 and 500 of the Companies Act 2006 set legal requirements in relation to the auditor's right
to obtain information. right to obtain information.*

5   Although the auditor is responsible for communicating matters required by this ISA (UK), management also has a responsibility to communicate matters of governance interest to those charged with governance. Communication by the auditor does not relieve management of this responsibility. Similarly, communication by management with those charged with governance of matters that the auditor is required to communicate does not relieve the auditor of the responsibility to also communicate them. Communication of these matters by management may, however, affect the form or timing of the auditor's communication with those charged with governance.

6   Clear communication of specific matters required to be communicated by ISAs (UK) is an integral part of every audit. ISAs (UK) do not, however, require the auditor to perform procedures specifically to identify any other matters to communicate with those charged with governance.

7   Law or regulation may restrict the auditor's communication of certain matters with those charged with governance. For example, laws or regulations may specifically prohibit a communication, or other action, that might prejudice an investigation by an appropriate authority into an actual, or suspected, illegal act. In some circumstances, potential conflicts between the auditor's obligations of confidentiality and obligations to communicate may be complex. In such cases, the auditor may consider obtaining legal advice.

Effective Date

8   This ISA (UK) is effective for audits of financial statements for periods commencing on or after 17 June 2016. Earlier adoption is permitted.

Objectives

9   The objectives of the auditor are:

(a)   To communicate clearly with those charged with governance the responsibilities of the auditor in relation to the financial statement audit, and an overview of the planned scope and timing of the audit;

(b)   To obtain from those charged with governance information relevant to the audit;

(c)   To provide those charged with governance with timely observations arising from the audit that are significant and relevant to their responsibility to oversee the financial reporting process; and

(d)   To promote effective two-way communication between the auditor and those charged with governance.

Definitions

10   For purposes of the ISAs (UK), the following terms have the meanings attributed below:

(a)   Those charged with governance – The person(s) or organization(s) (e.g., a corporate trustee) with responsibility for overseeing the strategic direction of the entity and obligations related to the accountability of the entity. This includes overseeing the financial reporting process. For some entities in some jurisdictions, those charged with governance may include management personnel, for example, executive members of a governance board of a private or public sector entity, or an owner-manager. For discussion of the diversity of governance structures, see paragraphs A1–A8.

> In the UK, those charged with governance include the directors (executive and non-executive) of a company and the members of an audit committee where one exists. For other types of entity it usually includes equivalent persons such as the partners, proprietors, committee of management or trustees.

(b) Management – The person(s) with executive responsibility for the conduct of the entity's operations. For some entities in some jurisdictions, management includes some or all of those charged with governance, for example, executive members of a governance board, or an owner-manager.

In the UK, management will not normally include non-executive directors.

Requirements

Those Charged with Governance

The auditor shall determine the appropriate person(s) within the entity's governance structure with whom to communicate. (Ref: Para. A1–A4)   **11**

For audits of financial statements of public interest entities, if the entity does not have an audit committee, the additional report to the audit committee required by paragraph 16R-2 shall be submitted to the body performing equivalent functions within the entity.   **11R-1**

Communication with a Subgroup of Those Charged with Governance

If the auditor communicates with a subgroup of those charged with governance, for example, an audit committee, or an individual, the auditor shall determine whether the auditor also needs to communicate with the governing body. (Ref: Para. A5–A7)   **12**

When All of Those Charged with Governance Are Involved in Managing the Entity

In some cases, all of those charged with governance are involved in managing the entity, for example, a small business where a single owner manages the entity and no one else has a governance role. In these cases, if matters required by this ISA (UK) are communicated with person(s) with management responsibilities, and those person(s) also have governance responsibilities, the matters need not be communicated again with those same person(s) in their governance role. These matters are noted in paragraph 16(c). The auditor shall nonetheless be satisfied that communication with person(s) with management responsibilities adequately informs all of those with whom the auditor would otherwise communicate in their governance capacity. (Ref: Para. A8)   **13**

Matters to Be Communicated

The Auditor's Responsibilities in Relation to the Financial Statement Audit

The auditor shall communicate with those charged with governance the responsibilities of the auditor in relation to the financial statement audit, including that: **14**

(a) The auditor is responsible for forming and expressing an opinion on the financial statements that have been prepared by management[1b] with the oversight of those charged with governance; and

(b) The audit of the financial statements does not relieve management or those charged with governance of their responsibilities. (Ref: Para. A9–A10)

[1b] *In the UK, those charged with governance are responsible for the preparation of the financial statements.*

Planned Scope and Timing of the Audit

15   The auditor shall communicate with those charged with governance an overview of the planned scope and timing of the audit, which includes communicating about the significant risks identified by the auditor. (Ref: Para. A11–A16)

> When the auditor is required or decides to communicate key audit matters in accordance with ISA (UK) 701,[1c] the overview of the planned scope and timing of the audit shall also include communicating about the most significant assessed risks of material misstatement (whether or not due to fraud) identified by the auditor, including those that had the greatest effect on: the overall audit strategy; the allocation of resources in the audit; and directing the efforts of the engagement team.

Significant Findings from the Audit

16   The auditor shall communicate with those charged with governance: (Ref: Para. A17–A18)

(a)   The auditor's views about significant qualitative aspects of the entity's accounting practices, including accounting policies, accounting estimates and financial statement disclosures. When applicable, the auditor shall explain to those charged with governance why the auditor considers a significant accounting practice, that is acceptable under the applicable financial reporting framework, not to be most appropriate to the particular circumstances of the entity; (Ref: Para. A19–A20)

(b)   Significant difficulties, if any, encountered during the audit; (Ref: Para. A21)

(c)   Unless all of those charged with governance are involved in managing the entity:

(i)   Significant matters arising during the audit that were discussed, or subject to correspondence, with management; and (Ref: Para. A22)

(ii)   Written representations the auditor is requesting;

(d)   Circumstances that affect the form and content of the auditor's report, if any; and (Ref: Para. A23–A25)

(e)   Any other significant matters arising during the audit that, in the auditor's professional judgment, are relevant to the oversight of the financial reporting process. (Ref: Para. A26–A28)

Entities that Report on Application of the UK Corporate Governance Code

16-1   In the case of entities that are required,[1d] and those that choose voluntarily, to report on how they have applied the UK Corporate Governance Code, or to explain why they have not, the auditor shall communicate to the audit committee the information that the auditor believes will be relevant to: (Ref: Para. A20-1)

● The board (in the context of fulfilling its responsibilities under Code provisions C.1.1, C.1.3, C.2.1, C.2.2 and C.2.3) and, where applicable, the audit committee (in the context of fulfilling its responsibilities under Code provision C.3.4); and

● The audit committee (in the context of fulfilling its responsibilities under Code provision C.3.2) in order to understand the rationale and the supporting evidence the auditor has relied on when making significant professional judgments in the course of the audit and in reaching an opinion on the financial statements.

[1c] *Paragraphs 30–31 of ISA (UK) 700 (Revised June 2016)*, Forming an Opinion and Reporting on Financial Statements, *set out the requirements to apply ISA (UK) 701*, Communicating Key Audit Matters in the Independent Auditor's Report.

[1d] *In the UK, these include companies with a premium listing of equity shares regardless of whether they are incorporated in the UK or elsewhere.*

If not already covered by communications under paragraphs 15, 16 and 16R-2 of this ISA (UK) and paragraph 25 of ISA (UK) 570 (Revised June 2016), this information shall include the auditor's views: (Ref: Para. A20-2–A20-5)

(a) About business risks relevant to financial reporting objectives, the application of materiality and the implications of their judgments in relation to these for the overall audit strategy, the audit plan and the evaluation of misstatements identified;

(b) On the significant accounting policies (both individually and in aggregate);

(c) On management's valuations of the entity's material assets and liabilities and the related disclosures provided by management;

(d) Without expressing an opinion on the effectiveness of the entity's system of internal control as a whole, and based solely on the audit procedures performed in the audit of the financial statements, about:

    (i) The effectiveness of the entity's system of internal control relevant to risks that may affect financial reporting; and

    (ii) Other risks arising from the entity's business model and the effectiveness of related internal controls to the extent, if any, the auditor has obtained an understanding of these matters;

(e) About the robustness of the directors' assessment of the principal risks facing the entity, including those that would threaten its business model, future performance, solvency or liquidity and its outcome, including the related disclosures in the annual report confirming that they have carried out such an assessment and describing those risks and explaining how they are being managed or mitigated (in accordance with Code provision C.2.1);

(f) About the directors' explanation in the annual report as to how they have assessed the prospects of the entity, over what period they have done so and why they consider that period to be appropriate (in accordance with Code provision C.2.2), and their statements:

    (i) in the financial statements, as to whether they considered it appropriate to adopt the going concern basis of accounting in preparing them, including any related disclosures identifying any material uncertainties to the entity's ability to continue to do so over a period of at least twelve months from the date of approval of the financial statements (in accordance with Code provision C.1.3); and

    (ii) in the annual report as to whether they have a reasonable expectation that the entity will be able to continue in operation and meet its liabilities as they fall due over the period of their assessment, including any related disclosures drawing attention to any necessary qualifications or assumptions (in accordance with Code provision C.2.2); and

(g) On any other matters identified in the course of the audit that the auditor believes will be relevant to the board or the audit committee in the context of fulfilling their responsibilities referred to above.

The auditor shall include with this communication sufficient explanation to enable the audit committee to understand the context within which the auditor's views relating to the matters in paragraph (d) above are expressed, including the extent to which the auditor has developed an understanding of these matters in the course of the audit and, if not already communicated to the audit committee, that the audit included consideration of internal control relevant to the preparation of the financial statements only in order to design audit procedures that are appropriate in the circumstances, and not for the purpose of expressing an opinion on the effectiveness of internal control.

Public Interest Entities

For audits of financial statements of public interest entities, the auditor shall submit an additional report to the audit committee of the entity explaining the results of the audit carried out and shall at least:

    16R-2

(a) Include the declaration of independence required by paragraph 17R-1(a);

(b) Identify each key audit partner(s)[1e] involved in the audit;

(c) Where the auditor has made arrangements for any of the auditor's activities to be conducted by another firm[1f] that is not a member of the same network, or has used the work of external experts, the report shall indicate that fact and shall confirm that the auditor received a confirmation from the other firm and/or the external expert regarding their independence;

(d) Describe the nature, frequency and extent of communication with the audit committee or the body performing equivalent functions within the entity, the management body and the administrative or supervisory body of the entity, including the dates of meetings with those bodies;

(e) Include a description of the scope and timing of the audit;

(f) Where more than one auditor has been appointed, describe the distribution of tasks among the auditors;

(g) Describe the methodology used, including which categories of the balance sheet have been directly verified and which categories have been verified based on system and compliance testing, including an explanation of any substantial variation in the weighting of system and compliance testing when compared to the previous year, even if the previous year's audit was carried out by another firm;

(h) Disclose the quantitative level of materiality applied to perform the audit for the financial statements as a whole and where applicable the materiality level or levels for particular classes of transactions, account balances or disclosures, and disclose the qualitative factors which were considered when setting the level of materiality;

(i) Report and explain judgments about events or conditions identified in the course of the audit that may cast significant doubt on the entity's ability to continue as a going concern and whether they constitute a material uncertainty, and provide a summary of all guarantees, comfort letters, undertakings of public intervention and other support measures that have been taken into account when making a going concern assessment;

(j) Report on any significant deficiencies in the entity's or, in the case of consolidated financial statements, the parent undertaking's internal financial control system, and/or in the accounting system. For each such significant deficiency, the additional report shall state whether or not the deficiency in question has been resolved by management;

(k) Report any significant matters involving actual or suspected non-compliance with laws and regulations or articles of association which were identified in the course of the audit, in so far as they are considered to be relevant in order to enable the audit committee to fulfil its tasks;

(l) Report the valuation methods[1g] applied to the various items in the annual or consolidated financial statements including any impact of changes of such methods;

(m) In the case of an audit of consolidated financial statements, explain the scope of consolidation and the exclusion criteria applied by the entity to the non-consolidated entities, if any, and whether those criteria applied are in accordance with the financial reporting framework;

(n) Where applicable, identify any audit work performed by component auditors in relation to an audit of consolidated financial statements other than by members of the same network to which the auditor of the consolidated financial statements belongs;

[1e] *'Key audit partner' is defined in paragraph 7D-1(d) of ISA (UK) 220 (Revised June 2016),* Quality Control for an Audit of Financial Statements.

[1f] *'Firm' is defined in ISA (UK) 220 (Revised June 2016) as a sole practitioner, partnership or corporation or other entity of professional accountants.*

[1g] *ISA (UK) 330 (Revised June 2016),* The Auditor's Responses to Assessed Risks, *paragraph 19R-1 deals with the auditor's responsibility to assess the valuation methods applied, including any impact of changes of such methods.*